WHAT PEOPLE HAVE SAID ABOUT
THE TIMEWASTER LETTERS

I took the manuscript into the lavatory. . . . So engrossing and funny was the collection, I remained in the toilet for an entire hour. I believe my neighbours may now consider me strange, because of the peels of loud raucous laughter emanating from my "little boy's room." It is truly brilliant.

SIMON PEGG, *Hot Fuzz, Shaun of the Dead*

Funny eccentric Britisher Robin Cooper writes very funny letters of ludicrous inquiry. Read this, laugh, and feel better about yourself for using your time so wisely.

BOB ODENKIRK, *Mr. Show*

Probably the funniest book you'll read this year.

The Guardian

This is the funniest book I have ever read.

MATT LUCAS, *Little Britain*

I laughed so much I hurt myself—and others.

DAVID WALLIAMS, *Little Britain*

Don't read this book in public. You will laugh very hard and very loud and people will think you're crazy. We recommend reading it exclusively in your shed. WE LOVE THIS BOOOOOOK!!!!!!

TIM AND ERIC, *Tim & Eric Awesome Show*

Terribly funny. . . . A genuinely funny book is as rare nowadays as a North Korean chat show. Mr. Cooper is a real find.

The Independent

Not many books have me laughing out loud, shouting F**k off! in disbelief. This one did.

MARTIN FREEMAN, *The Hitchhiker's Guide to the Galaxy*

Comic genius.

Daily Mail

I have WASTED two hours this morning weeing myself in hysterics at the book. . . . It's completely brilliant.

STEPHANIE MERRITT, *The Observer*

THE TIMEWASTER LETTERS

Robin Cooper

CHICAGO
REVIEW
PRESS

Cover design: Sarah Olson
Interior design: Burville-Riley

First published in Great Britian in 2004 by
Michael O'Mara Books Limited
9 Lion Yard
Tremadoc Road
London SW4 7NQ
Copyright © Robert Popper 2004
All rights reserved
First U.S. edition published in 2008 by
Chicago Review Press Incorporated
814 North Franklin Street
Chicago, IL 60610
ISBN 978-1-55652-755-5
Printed and bound in the United States of America
9 8 7 6 5 4 3 2 1

Dedicated to the memory of Hambles

ACKNOWLEDGEMENTS

Hearty thanks to the following, for helping me with the physical and actual making of this book:
Simon Trewin
Lindsay Davies
Kate Gribble
Marc Burville-Riley

Additional (but no less hearty) thanks to:
My parents, Jonny, Claire, Peter and Sarah ('hebbo'), Geoff Atkinson, Emma Benson, Jonathan Bloom, James Brown, Matthew Clayton, Melanie Coupland, Paula Davie, Dan Davies, Philip Davis, Mark Freeland, Simon Gallant, Natasha Galloway, Alex Godfrey, Simon Henwood, Edmund Hitchcock, everyone at *Jack* magazine, Steve Lazarus, Cat Ledger, Jon Link, Matt Lucas, Cathy Mason, Stephanie Merritt, Spencer Millman, Barney Pinny, Neil Pepin, the postman, Sonia Pugh, Faye Webber, David Whitehouse, everyone who was kind enough to provide a quote, everyone who ever replied to my letters, and anyone else I may have forgotten but didn't mean to (forget).

www.robincooper.co.uk

Robin Cooper
Brondesbury Villas
London

Windrush Mill Garden Catalogue
Ryan House
Grove Street
Cheltenham
Glos
GL50 3LZ

6th April 1999

Dear Sir/Madam,

I was recently sent a copy of your Quality Garden Catalogue (Spring 99), and I'd like to congratulate you on such a fine brochure.

I have worked as a landscape gardener for 15 years and have never seen such a fine array of items to perk up the garden. Well done!

You may be interested to know that I design garden-related products. I have an entire range of scarecrows made entirely from beef. They are based on Roman themes, such as 'The Storming of Thebes' and 'Brutus Avenged'. I wonder if you would be interested in looking at the designs to put in your new catalogue.

I look forward to your reply, and once again, bravo!

Best wishes,

Robin Cooper

THE QUALITY GARDEN CATALOGUE

Ryan House, Grove Street, Cheltenham, Glos GL50 3LZ

Robin Cooper
Brondesbury Villas
London

15th April 99

Dear Robin

My name is Emma Hutt and I am Johnnie Vizor's assistant at Windrush Mill. He has asked me to write to you to thank you for your letter and compliments. We would be very interested to see the scarcrows made of beef (?). Please send details of the products to the above address including any pictures and the cost prices.
I look forward to hearing from you.

With regards

Emma Hutt
Buying assistant

Robin Cooper
Brondesbury Villas
London

Emma Hutt
Windrush Mill Garden Catalogue
Ryan House
Grove Street
Cheltenham
Glos
GL50 3LZ

20th April 1999

Dear Emma,

Many thanks for your letter of the 15th April 1999.

I was delighted that you wrote back to me (on behalf of Johnnie Vizor).

As requested I am enclosing copies of my latest designs for my scarecrows, based on Roman themes. They can currently be seen in my front garden, should you care to visit.

I was a bit confused when you mentioned that my designs were made of 'beef'. I can only assume I made a spelling mistake on the machine. It should of course have read 'beel'.

For your interest, each model is priced at £21.99.

I look forward to hearing what you think of my designs, and would like to, once again, congratulate you on your magnificent brochure.

Yours sincerely,

Robin Cooper

#1: 'LUCRETIA IN DISMAY'

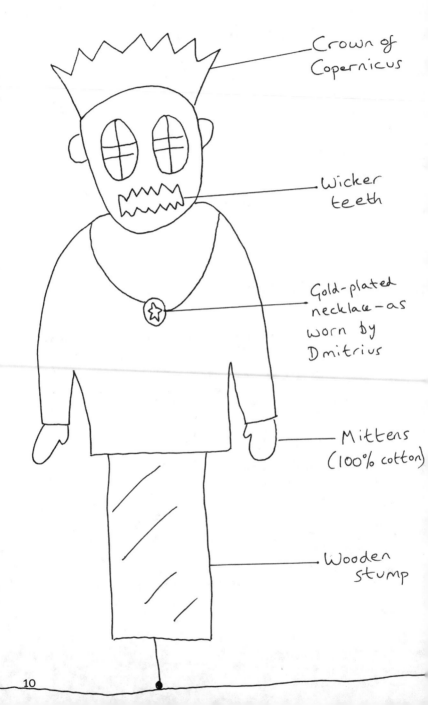

Crown of Copernicus

Wicker teeth

Gold-plated necklace – as worn by Dmitrius

Mittens (100% cotton)

Wooden Stump

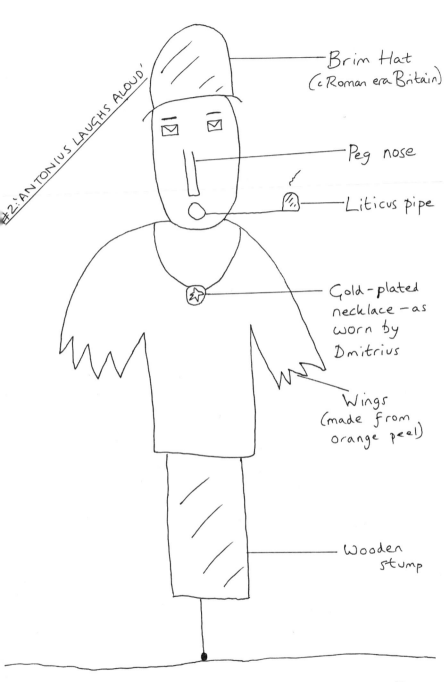

#2: ANTONIUS LAUGHS ALOUD'

Brim Hat
(c Roman era Britain)

Peg nose

Liticus pipe

Gold-plated
necklace — as
worn by
Dmitrius

Wings
(made from
orange peel)

Wooden
stump

11

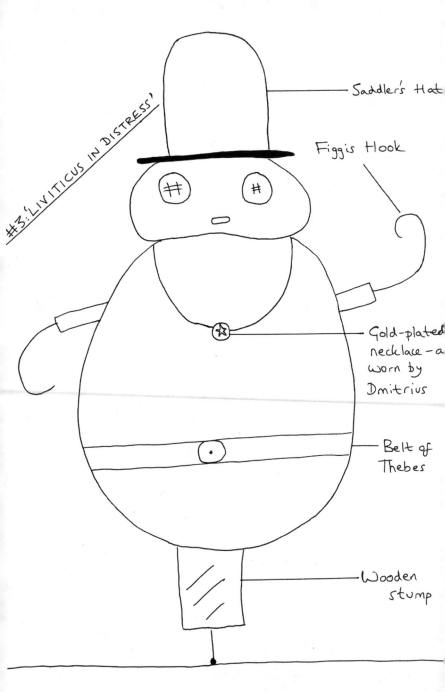

Saddler's Hat

Figgis Hook

Gold-plated necklace – a worn by Dmitrius

Belt of Thebes

Wooden stump

THE QUALITY GARDEN CATALOGUE

Ryan House, Grove Street, Cheltenham, Glos GL50 3LZ

Robin Cooper
Brondesbury Villas
London

26th April 99

Dear Robin

Thank you for your letter and designs for the beel scarecrows. We are at present looking at the Spring/Summer 2000 range but after long consideration we feel this product is not suitable on this occasion.

Thank you for taking the time to send us details of your products and please bear us in mind with any new products.

With regards

Emma Hutt

Emma Hutt
Windrush Mill Garden Catalogue
Ryan House
Grove Street
Cheltenham
Glos
GL50 3LZ

27th April 1999

Dear Emma,

Many thanks for your letter. I was disappointed that you have decided not to go with my scarecrows – but not as disappointed as they will be when I tell them!

You kindly mentioned that I should bear you in mind with any new products I may have. Well, I have recently been working on a new design, which I refer to as *The Taupendulator*, (drawings enclosed).

Like my scarecrows, *The Taupendulator* is designed to ward off garden birds and gulls. It's once again based on Roman themes, and you'll notice that it hearkens back to the days of Cassius, Dementicles and Julius of Thane.

The principle of *The Taupendulator* is quite simple. The product sits in the flower bed or vegetable patch, held down with rope. The opening is filled with a syrup (based on my own recipe – a mixture of camphor, petrol, iodine and cream) and left to stand for 24 hours. After this period, birds become naturally attracted to the odour, and fly in to investigate.

The Taupendulator works in a similar way to the Venus Fly Trap. Birds which rest on the 'lip' of the device trigger a set of springs inside, causing the 'mouth' of the product to clamp shut on the bird. The bird is then totally immersed in the syrup, which acts much like any quick-setting glue. Within 10-15 minutes the bird is completely immobilised, and can be disposed of (bag supplied).

I am sure *The Taupendulator* is something that would fit nicely in your excellent garden catalogue, and feel confident it could really catch on. I hope you enjoy my designs, and look forward to hearing from you.

With very best wishes,

Robin Cooper

THE TAUPENDULATOR:

Design by
Robin Cooper

PRICE: £41.99

① Taupendulator fixed in flower bed/vegetable patch by ropes.

Taupendulator

② Syrup (camphor, petrol, iodine, cream mix) poured in.

Syrup

Jug

Taupendulator

③ After 24 hours, birds and gulls become attracted to odour, and fly in to investigate.

Bird

Taupendulator

④ Bird triggers lid to close, enveloping the bird. Wings are glued together.

Lid closed

Bird inside

Taupendulator

⑤ After 10-15 minutes, bird is disposed of in bag.

Bag containing immobilised bird

Taupendulator

15

THE QUALITY GARDEN CATALOGUE

Ryan House, Grove Street, Cheltenham, Glos GL50 3LZ

Robin Cooper
Brondesbury Villas
London

29th April 99

Dear Robin

Thank you for your letter and diagram. We regard ourselves as a bird friendly catalogue and feel that this product is particularly cruel to birds and thus in no way suitable to be considered for selection.

With regards

Emma Hutt

END OF CORRESPONDENCE

Robin Cooper
Brondesbury Villas
London

Sue Unstead
Commissioning Editor for Childrens' Books
Dorling Kindersley
9 Henrietta Street
London WC2E 8PS

30th April 1999

Dear Sue,

The other day, my youngest daughter, Lisa, looked up to me and said, "Daddy, does television really rot the soul?"

Lisa is only nine.

I think you can see what I'm getting at. Where is the world going that a nine-year old child should consider the potential for mind-dilution, caused by the so-called 'harmless' box in the corner (of the living room)?

That's why I have decided to write a book. It's called **Kelly Telly and his Smelly Belly**.

It's a children's book all about a television set called Kelly. The belly I refer to is the screen, and the reason it's 'smelly' is because it pumps out spurious filth dressed up as 'entertainment', destined for our children's eyes. It's basically a satire on the Me-Have-It-All-Remote-Control-TV-Times-Intanet-Generation.

I have some drawings of the characters, who include Kelly Telly, Lorna Duck and Sammy Hagar the local butcher.

I would love to send my sketches to you, as I feel the time is right for **Kelly Telly and his Smelly Belly**. I have already written 20 books in my life.

I look forward to hearing from you.

Fingers crossed.

Yours sincerely,

R. L. Co

Robin Cooper

Robin Cooper
Brondesbury Villas
London

04/05/99

Dear Robin

Thank you so much for your letter of 30th April and your proposal for a book entitled <u>Kelly Telly and his Smelly Belly</u>.

Unfortunately, we don't think that the idea fits into our publishing list at the moment. However, I wish you every success with your book.

Thank you for thinking of Dorling Kindersley.

Yours sincerely,

Sue Unstead
Category Publisher

Dorling Kindersley Limited
9 HENRIETTA STREET, COVENT GARDEN, LONDON WC2E 8PS

VAT number: 429 5337 34 · Registered in England no: 1177822 · Registered office: 9 Henrietta Street, London WC2E 8PS

Robin Cooper
Brondesbury Villas
London

Sue Unstead
Commissioning Editor for Childrens' Books
Dorling Kindersley
9 Henrietta Street
London WC2E 8PS

7th May 1999

Dear Sue,

Many thanks for your letter of the 4th May about my proposed book, **Kelly Telly and his Smelly Belly**. You're right. I read it again and it's not very good.

THAT IS WHY I HAVE DECIDED TO PUT MY BOOK THROUGH THE SHREDDER TONIGHT AT 9PM.

Anyway, I have another book to propose to you. It's called **Stanislav Humtovsky – the Sad Bureaucrat**. It's a tale of a Czech bookkeeper who is constantly bullied for his lack of personal hygiene. I think it has all the makings of a hit.

Here's an extract:

The wind tore through Proszca Square. Stanilslav Humtovsky buttoned up his coat and took a swig from his hip flask.

'Curse them!' He railed. 'Curse them all! Damn them to high heaven. Ignorant *Prosznovski*.'

A cat, its face twisted in hunger, scurried after a beetle amongst the city dustbins.

'Dirty beast! Filthy rag!'

Humtovsky leapt after it, squashing its tail underfoot. With a pained squeal and a flash of sharpened claws, the cat lunged at Humtovsky's ankles.

'Damned vermin!'

Humtovsky knelt down to examine the wound. Warm blood trickled between his fingers onto his shoe. Somewhere a radio played '*Little Olga*', a woman laughed, and an old man coughed and cleared his throat.

I'd love to know if **Stanislav Humtovsky – the Sad Bureaucrat** is the type of book you are looking for (it does have a happy ending). I look forward to hearing from you.

With very best wishes,

Robin Cooper

Robin Cooper

19

Robin Cooper
Brondesbury Villas
London

10/05/99

Dear Robin

Thank you for your letter of 7 May. I hope you didn't really put <u>Kelly Telly and his Smelly Belly</u> through the shredder. All creative work should be cherished, and you may have found luck with another publisher.

However, I would like to have a look at <u>Stanislav Humtovsky - the Sad Bureaucrat</u>. It is very difficult to grasp a picture of the book with such a small extract, and so I would like to see the full text if possible. When I have had a better look at the text I will be able to judge if it is suitable for Dorling Kindersley.

Thank you again for sending your ideas to Dorling Kindersley.

Yours sincerely,

Clare Lister
Editorial Co-ordinator

Dorling Kindersley Limited
9 HENRIETTA STREET, COVENT GARDEN, LONDON WC2E 8PS

VAT number: 429 5337 34 · Registered in England no: 1177822 · Registered office: 9 Henrietta Street, London WC2E 8PS

Robin Cooper
Brondesbury Villas
London

Clare Lister
Editorial Co-ordinator
Dorling Kindersley
9 Henrietta Street
London WC2E 8PS

26th May 1999

Dear Clare,

KAPOW! Sue Unstead has changed into Clare Lister!

It's nice to make your acquaintance and thank you for your letter.

I'm sad to say that I did go ahead with my plans and I shredded my book, **Kelly Belly and his Smelly Belly**. I did it in the garage, and I felt physically sick afterwards.

You wrote asking to see my latest children's book, **Stanislav Humtovsky – the Sad Bureaucrat**. Please don't be cross with me Clare. I shredded that one as well. I don't know why I did it – maybe I'm just a perfectionist?

Anyway, I have another book which is aimed at the 9-12 year old market. It's a pop-up book based on the life of the inventor, William Stanley Jr (1858-1916). It's called **William Stanley Jr (1858-1916), Inventor**.

As you may know, Stanley invented the induction coil, a device which has provided lighting for countless homes and offices all over the world. I bet Dorling Kindersley owe Stanley a bob or two!!!

My book covers his work with metal plating, alternating current and transformers. It also delves into his, at times difficult, personal life, and my account of Stanley's first marriage goes into very great detail.

I have a terrific feeling about this book – I just know the kids are gonna love it!

Would you like me to send you some samples? I'd hate to have to put **William Stanley Jr (1858-1916), Inventor** through the shredder.

I look forward to hearing from you.

Best wishes,

Robin Cooper

Robin Cooper
Brondesbury Villas
London

28/05/99

Dear Robin

Thank you very much for your letter of 26 May. It was very nice to hear from you again, although disappointing that you hadn't sent Stanislav Humtovsky - the Sad Bureaucrat. I was looking forward to reading it.

Your new idea sounds very interesting. However, I am not sure if 9-12 year olds would be interested in William Stanley Jr's first marriage. Some of the intimate details may be too old for this age group. However, I am loathe to criticise in case you shred this too.

Perhaps you can send me some of your text so that I could look through it.

Thank you again for writing to us, and for sharing your ideas with us. I look forward to hearing from you.

Yours sincerely,

Clare Lister
Editorial Co-ordinator

Dorling Kindersley Limited
9 Henrietta Street, Covent Garden, London WC2E 8PS

VAT number: 429 5337 34 · Registered in England no: 1177822 · Registered office: 9 Henrietta Street, London WC2E 8PS

Robin Cooper
Brondesbury Villas
London

Clare Lister
Editorial Co-ordinator
Dorling Kindersley
9 Henrietta Street
London WC2E 8PS

8th June 1999

Dear Clare,

Thank you for your letter of 28th May. I'm sorry I've taken so long to get back to you - I've been building a shed in the garden and it's taken up most of my time (and nearly put my back out!!!!!!!!!!).

I am enclosing, as requested, a sample of text from **William Stanley Jr (1858 – 1916), Inventor**.

You shed some doubts about its SUITABILITY for the age group (kids 9-12 year olds). I think it has enough excitement to really 'reel in' the kids (9-12).

Have a read, and tell me what you think.

Will you publish it Clare???

Best wishes,

Robin Cooper

Robin Cooper

CHAPTER THREE

William Stanley Jr woke with a shudder. The pain in the head of the inventor of the induction coil had refused to budge. He felt as if a parrot had laid its eggs inside his brain, then squawked a message of hatred at the top of its shrill, rasping voice.

'What a night,' he said, 'What a terrible, terrible night.'

Helen rolled over in her sleep. A dreadful thought came over Stanley. A thought so dark, so full of brooding menace, that it threatened to pour like thick, black treacle from the ceiling. It threatened to sully the early morning with its stubborn, stretching, stain.

'Wake up! Wake up!' he yelled, 'I know who murdered the priest!'

Helen didn't stir. Stanley, whose invention had provided electric light to thousands of office workers up and down the country, frowned.

'Wake up wife! Wake up I tell you! I have my proof!'

There was something about Helen's silence, the fact that her eyes were open, yet her body was still, that said something was not right. Stanley – the man whose very work had literally lit up people's lives – peered gingerly over at his new wife.

'Lord help me. She's dead.'

The police came a-knocking at midday.

'Open up!' they barked like a pack of hungry wolves with supper on their minds.

'I'm coming,' said Stanley. Stanley pulled on his bedclothes, clambered over his wife's limp body, and walked to the door.

'Open up will you!'

Master of the transformer, William Stanley Jr, unlocked the door. The click of its metal locks sounded like a million crickets in a field of dry wheat and barley.

In the landing stood Huntley and Breech, pride of the police department.

'We want a word with you,' said Huntley.

'I'm glad you came,' smiled Stanley, peeling a peach with a small, carving knife.

Robin Cooper
Brondesbury Villas
London

28/05/99

Dear Robin

Thank you for your letter of 8 June, and apologies for my late response. It has been very busy here.

I'm very sorry to hear that you have been working so tremendously hard in the garden. I do hope your back is okay.

I have read the extract you sent in from William Stanley Jr, Inventor, and although I did laugh and enjoy it very much, I do feel that it is a little too weird for us to publish. Perhaps this is because the extract was out of context. In future I suggest you send in a larger extract so that I can really understand what part of the story you have included.

Although I feel that this is not suitable for us at this time, I do NOT suggest you shred this material. Why not try sending your writing to another publisher? What doesn't suit us might very well suit them.

In the meantime, thank you for sending us your writing and ideas at Dorling Kindersley, and I look forward to hearing from you again.

Best wishes,

Clare Lister
Editorial Co-ordinator

Dorling Kindersley Limited
9 Henrietta Street, Covent Garden, London WC2E 8PS

VAT number: 429 5337 34 · Registered in England no: 1177822 · Registered office: 9 Henrietta Street, London WC2E 8PS

Clare Lister
Editorial Co-ordinator
Dorling Kindersley
9 Henrietta Street
London WC2E 8PS

30th June 1999

Dear Clare,

Greetings along with many thanks for your letter.

Have you invented the Time Machine? I ask this because your response to my letter was dated 28th May, whereas my letter was sent to you on 8th June. I can only assume you either leapt back in time or are completely psychic!!!!!!

Anyway, I am sorry to learn that **William Stanley Jr (1858 – 1916), Inventor**, didn't do it for you. Perhaps I should have sent you the bit when he actually invented the induction coil.

I take your advice about sending my writing elsewhere, but I want to keep sending your company IDEAS, as I believe we have built up a good working relationship so far.

So, I have a new idea for the Kids (or 'The Kidz' as they all call them these days). It's a trilogy called **Mrs Mallett and Her Catty**. It's all about an elderly woman (she's 108) and the adventures of her magic cat, Catty. Catty can not only talk, but can sew as well. Each episode features Catty sewing or making an embroidery of an imaginary world. Catty tries to get Mrs Mallett to enter the mystical world with her, but sadly Mrs Mallett is infirm and has to stay at home.

Catty embarks on a series of amazing journeys all on her own:

Book One: Catty and Dr Finch:
Catty knits a woollen world where speech is forbidden and children are forced to live in caves. The whole place is run by the evil Dr Finch. In the end Catty defeats Dr Finch by letting him suckle on her until he falls asleep. Catty then burns Dr Finch in front of the villagers.

Book Two: Catty and Finbaloid:
Catty weaves a pattern of an underwater world and then goes there. She meets the evil Finbaloid, a two-headed man who has the world at ransom because he has the most amount of nuclear energy ever. In the end Catty gets Finbaloid to suckle and whilst Finbaloid is sleeping, Catty burns him.

Book Three: Catty and Catty Mark II:
A robot Catty (Catty II) has been made and Catty (I) is not happy. Catty (I) gets Catty II to suckle on her and whilst Catty II is fast asleep, Catty (I) burns her. There is a good twist at the end in which all the baddies (Dr Finch and Finbaloid) come back with anger in their eyes…

I have included a picture of Catty here. I hope you like the idea.
I look forward to hearing from you soon.

Best wishes,

Robin Cooper

Robin Cooper
Brondesbury Villas
London

19/07/99

Dear Robin

Thank you for your letter of 30 June. I haven't invented the Time
Machine, but I seem to have dated some of my letters wrongly. Many
apologies for this.

I was most amused by your latest idea called Mrs Mallett and Her Catty.
The trilogy sounds fantastic but I am worried about a couple of points.
Firstly the idea of the 'baddies' suckling on Catty is a slightly disturbing
image, which I think would be unsuitable for a children's book. In
publishing we do have to be careful which ideas we put into a child's
mind.

I also think that the idea of the robot Catty in the third of the stories is
good but one I have seen before, perhaps in Superman?

Overall I was impressed with the stories, but feel they need more
development and thought. Mrs Mallett sounds like a terrific character.
Perhaps she deserves more of a role.

Your drawing of Catty gave me a good idea of the cat, but I would suggest
that you leave the illustrations to an illustrator.

Many thanks again for your ideas and thoughts.

Best wishes,

Clare Lister
Editorial Co-ordinator

Dorling Kindersley Limited
9 HENRIETTA STREET, COVENT GARDEN, LONDON WC2E 8PS

VAT number: 429 5337 34 · Registered in England no: 1177822 · Registered office: 9 Henrietta Street, London WC2E 8PS

Robin Cooper
Brondesbury Villas
London

Clare Lister
Editorial Co-ordinator
Dorling Kindersley
9 Henrietta Street
London WC2E 8PS

3rd August 1999

Dear Clare,

Thank you for your reply to my letter about **Mrs Mallett and Her Catty**. I was heartened (pleased) by your generally favourable comments about it.

OK, so you're not convinced it is the ONE for you. Well, believe it or not, I do have another idea for a great book for all the kids out there – and adults if they choose to read it !!!!!

It's called **Guntaarsyan Hip-Lun-Mivvin & Mr Taylor**. It's all about the antics of a self-replicating moth (Guntaarsyan Hip-Lun-Mivvin) and his survivalist master (Mr Taylor).

Mr Taylor takes Guntaarsyan Hip-Lun-Mivvin on holiday (Centreparks). Unfortunately Guntaarsyan Hip-Lun-Mivvin falls in the pool and swallows some chlorine. This has the side effect of making him immediately self-replicate, and soon the pool area is full of thousands and thousands of Guntaarsyan Hip-Lun-Mivvins. Mr Taylor has to convince the manager not to have his Guntaarsyan Hip-Lun-Mivvins exterminated.

But will he (Mr Taylor) succeed?…

I plan to make **Guntaarsyan Hip-Lun-Mivvin & Mr Taylor** in the form of a POP UP book for extra 3D interactive effect. Perhaps we could also include a CD Rom that tells children all about moths (their habitat, feeding etc.). Maybe we could get sponsorship from Centreparks to fund this book.

Do you want me to phone Centreparks or would it be best if you did it?

I look forward to hearing from you.

Best wishes,

Robin Cooper

Robin Cooper

Robin Cooper
Brondesbury Villas
London

13/08/99

Dear Robin

Thank you for your letter of 3 August. I am impressed at the quick
turnover of ideas that you seem to possess for children's books. However,
I do feel that you should perhaps pick your best idea and try to improve on
that with greater attention to detail, rather than flitting between ideas.
Each individual book takes a great deal of work and time.

Your latest idea, Guntaarsyan Hip-Lun-Mivvin and Mr Taylor, was even
more weird and wonderful than the others. It did make me laugh and I
can envisage it as a book, but I don't think that Dorling Kindersley are the
right publishers for you. Our fiction department is quite small and tends
to produce many licensed books. Therefore I would suggest that you
purchase, or borrow from your local library, the *Writer's and Artist's
Yearbook* published by A&C Black every year. I think that you will find this
book very helpful as it outlines the publishing process in detail.

Thank you again for sending in your ideas to us, and I do wish you every
success in finding the right publisher for you.

Best wishes,

Clare Lister
Editorial Co-ordinator

Dorling Kindersley Limited
9 HENRIETTA STREET, COVENT GARDEN, LONDON WC2E 8PS

VAT number: 429 5337 34 · Registered in England no: 1177822 · Registered office: 9 Henrietta Street, London WC2E 8PS

Clare Lister
Editorial Co-ordinator
Dorling Kindersley
9 Henrietta Street
London WC2E 8PS

17th August 1999

Dear Clare,

Thank you with all my heart for your reply on the 13th August to my letter which I sent to you on the 3rd August.

My initial reaction was one of DELIGHT when you said "I (you) can envisage it **(Guntaarsyan Hip-Lun-Mivvin & Mr Taylor)** as a book", but my euphoria turned to DISTRESS when you added "I (you) don't think that Dorling Kindersley are the right publishers for you (me)".

I shredded the entire work. It took one minute and twenty seconds to destroy three months work.

Anyway, my wife told me not to give up, so I suggest a solution. I think it is time for us to set up a MEETING. I will bring along my 'Catalogue of Ideas' (there are 74 at my last count) and you can flick through the 'Catalogue' until you find the book you want to publish.

The ideas range from factual tomes - **'One Hundred and Twenty Four Thousand Nine Hundred and Six Hundreds and Thousands' (A Brief History of Cake Decorations)'** to religious works, **'Jason and Michelle Return to the Lord'**, as well as loads of brilliant ideas for children's books.

Please write back with a date and time as I do not have a (tele)phone. Also, will it be alright for me to bring my dogs along as well?

I look forward to hearing and then seeing from you.

Best wishes,

Robin Cooper

Robin Cooper

PS - I cannot make the 25th August as my wife is having her ankle x-rayed that day.

Robin Cooper
Brondesbury Villas
London

Clare Lister
Editorial Co-ordinator
Dorling Kindersley
9 Henrietta Street
London WC2E 8PS

9th September 1999

Dear Clare,

I trust that you are well.

I haven't heard from you since my last letter. Are you OK?

If you recall, we were trying to secure a MEETING so that you can really see my work in full.

I look forward to your reply.

Best wishes,

Robin Cooper

Robin Cooper

Robin Cooper
Brondesbury Villas
London

13/08/99

Dear Robin

Thank you for your letters of 17 August and 9 September respectively, and my sincerest apologies for not having responded sooner. I have been inundated with letters and we have been extremely busy preparing for the Frankfurt Book Fair.

In your letter of 17 August you demonstrated your perseverance and suggested a meeting. However, I really must reiterate that although your ideas do sound fabulous, Dorling Kindersley may not be the right forum for them. Our fiction department is small and we concentrate on licensed books such as Star Wars, Lego and Disney. I will speak again with my seniors in the fiction department, and I have copied our correspondence to them, but I do suggest you approach another children's publisher too.

I will be in touch again should my seniors in the fiction department show interest.

Until then, best of luck.

Best wishes,

Clare Lister
Editorial Co-ordinator

Dorling Kindersley Limited
9 HENRIETTA STREET, COVENT GARDEN, LONDON WC2E 8PS

VAT number: 429 5337 34 • Registered in England no: 1177822 • Registered office: 9 Henrietta Street, London WC2E 8PS

Robin Cooper
Brondesbury Villas
London

Martin Westwood
Chief Executive
Madame Tussauds
Marylebone Road
London NW1 5LR

1st July 1999

Dear Martin,

I understand your museum does waxworks of people like dignitaries and so forth.

I may not be a dignitary myself but I am dignified. Here's the proof:

1) I always get out of bed before 10am
2) I never raise my voice at women
3) I have never punished an animal with a stick

Would you do a waxwork of me?

I've been told I look rather like the Roman Emperor Augustus. Stick me in a toga and bingo! No one would know the difference. (It'll be our secret, Martin.)

Please inform me of the date and time of my modelling session.

Yours sincerely,

Robin Cooper

Mr. Robin Cooper
Brondesbury Villas
LONDON

MADAME TUSSAUD'S

2ⁿᵈ July, 1999

Marylebone Road
London NW1 5LR

Telephone: 0171-935 6861
Facsimile: 0171-465 0862

Dear Mr. Cooper,

Thank you for your letter of 1ˢᵗ July regarding the possibility of Madame Tussaud's producing a wax portrait of yourself. We do get a significant number of letters of this nature every year.

Whilst I appreciate your generous offer to sit for a portrait unfortunately Madame Tussaud's only has a very limited number of portraits that can be added to the exhibition in any one year.

We spend a considerable amount of time and effort selecting the personalities who will be approached, for example, this year we are including the Countess of Wessex, David Jason, Tim Henman and Billy Connolly. The focus of Madame Tussaud's exhibitions is on individuals who have earned a place in the public eye for a variety of reasons. We are not in the position to offer time for a sitting to anyone other than those who have gained widespread recognition both in this country and even internationally.

I know that this will be a disappointment to you but I hope you will appreciate our difficulties. Certainly, the research which we undertake with our visitors indicates that in the main we feature the personalities that our visitors hope to see.

Kind regards.

Yours sincerely,

Martin Westwood
General Manager

END OF CORRESPONDENCE

An attraction in
The Tussauds Group Limited
Registered No. 215035 in London
Registered Office: York Court,
Allsop Place, London NW1 5LR

Robin Cooper
Brondesbury Villas
London

Mr T D Wemyss
British Secondary Metals Association
Sandford Court
Lichfield
Staffs.
WS13 6QA

Dear Mr Wemyss,

I'll be blunt. It seems to me that your organisation is suffering from an extreme lack of self-confidence. I think you know what I'm talking about.

Yes, your name, The British <u>Secondary</u> Metals Association. Why 'secondary'? Come on Mr Wemyss, there's no need to talk yourselves down. Remember – you're the <u>best</u>. You're <u>Number One</u>.

I suggest a solution. Rename yourselves The British <u>Primary</u> Metals Association at once, and I assure you that things will really start looking up.

Let me know what you think.

Chin up.

R. Li C

Robin Cooper

· **B** · **S** · **M** · **A** ·

BRITISH SECONDARY METALS ASSOCIATION
Sandford Court, Sandford Street, Lichfield, Staffordshire WS13 6QA

9th July 1999

Mr R Cooper
Brondesbury Villas
London

Dear Mr Cooper

I thank you for your undated letter regarding the name of the British Secondary Metals Association – why secondary?

Secondary is to denote the difference that exists from primary metal. Primary metal is produced from virgin ore, and secondary metals are produced from a material that has had a previously finished state, namely non-ferrous scrap metal.

Hoping this clarifies the situation, and that you can be assured that this Association considers itself number 1 when addressing matters relating to non-ferrous <u>secondary</u> metals, and therefore we see no need to amend the name of the Association as suggested by yourself.

Yours sincerely

KLloyd

p.p. Duncan Wemyss
<u>Executive Director</u>

END OF CORRESPONDENCE

Robin Cooper
Brondesbury Villas
London

Mr J W Kendall
British Peanut Council Ltd
Haconsfield
Hetherselt
Norfolk

8th July 1999

Dear Mr Kendall,

I am trying to get support for my latest business venture, and feel that your organisation might be able to help.

I am setting up a new service that will revolutionize office lunchbreaks. Here's how it works:

By fusing together thousands and thousands of peanuts, I have created a 'peanut suit' (jacket, tie, trousers, waistcoat etc.), which I can wear.

Once inside the suit I visit offices and workplaces during lunch hours. Office workers then buy coupons from me – at £1 a piece – each representing 5 minutes of snack time.

I then run around the office shouting "Mr Peanut! Mr Peanut!" while workers nibble at me for as long as their coupons allow.

You've got to admit, this idea has to be a winner. I also plan to bring this scheme to schools and, eventually, hospitals.

I'd be grateful if The British Peanut Council would send me a letter outlining your support. This would really help open many (office) doors.

I thank you in advance and promise I will not forget you. I will visit your premises on Thursday July 29th at 1:00pm, and reward each of your staff with free coupons up to the value of 10 minutes nibbling time.

I await your response.

Yours sincerely,

Robin Cooper

BRITISH PEANUT COUNCIL

"Promoting and protecting the interests of the British Peanut industry"

Please reply c/o:

Michael Dalton
Percy Dalton's Famous Peanut
Co. Ltd.
Old Ford Works
Dace Road
London E3 2PE

MJD/JC

12th July 1999

Robin Cooper, Esq.,
Brundesbury Villas,
London.

Dear Sir,

Your letter addressed to our Secretary Mr John Kendall has been passed by him to me for response.

I don't believe that the Peanut Council will be in a position to do as you request but nevertheless I will see that the marketing committee has a copy of your letter and I will also see that it is circulated in our next newsletter to members.

Yours faithfully
THE BRITISH PEANUT COUNCIL

Michael Dalton

END OF CORRESPONDENCE

Robin Cooper
Brondesbury Villas
London

Dr J S Buchanan
British Halibut Association
Manse Road
Overton
Roslin
Midlothian

8th July 1999

Dear Doc,

I am writing to tell you that last night my wife cooked me a piece of halibut.

It was bloody lovely.

Thought you might like to know.

Best wishes,

Robin C

Robin Cooper

BRITISH HALIBUT
ASSOCIATION

Please reply to:
Dr. J. S. Buchanan
BHA Secretary/Administrator

Robin Cooper,
Brondesbury Villas
London

13th July, 1999

Dear Mr. Cooper,

It was a delight to get your letter last Friday. Thank you for taking the trouble to write.

I have sent a copy of your letter to the board of directors of the Association.

As it happens, I too had a halibut steak on Saturday at the Oyster Catcher Pub by Otter Ferry and it was blooming marvellous.

We are on target with our production plans and should have 200,000 juveniles ready for ongrowing next year.

Yours sincerely

Jim Buchanan

Jim Buchanan
BHA Secretary/Administrator

END OF CORRESPONDENCE

38

Robin Cooper
Brondesbury Villas
London

Mr E H Thorne
Association of Beekeeping Appliance Manufacturers
Beehive Works
Lincs. LN3 5LA

12ᵗʰ July 1999

Dear Mr Thorne,

I think we all know that bees make honey. We take that as a given. However, how many of us know that wasps make mustard?

Although more bitter in taste than say, Dijon mustard, wasp mustard, or 'Waspard', makes a pleasant and healthy accompaniment to lamb, beef and even turkey.

I have been researching the mustard-producing properties of wasps for the past 9 years, and have come up with a fool-proof and cost-effective way to produce large quantities of Waspard.

Here's how it all works:

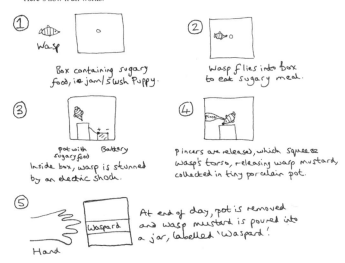

① Wasp — Box containing sugary food, ie jam/swsh Puppy.

② Wasp flies into box to eat sugary meal.

③ pot with sugary food   Battery — Inside box, wasp is stunned by an electric shock.

④ pincers are released, which squeeze wasp's torso, releasing wasp mustard, collected in tiny porcelain pot.

⑤ Waspard — Hand — At end of day, pot is removed and wasp mustard is poured into a jar, labelled 'Waspard'.

It's really that simple.

I'm currently planning a huge marketing campaign for Waspard and wonder if you would object if I quoted you on my promotional material.

The first advert is going to print in three weeks' time and I have taken the liberty to include the following words from your good self:

"I eat Waspard straight from the jar"
E.H. Thorne
Assn of Beekeeping Appliance Manufacturers

Hope that's OK. If you have any objections, please do not hesitate to write back.

Yours sincerely,

Robin Cooper

E.H.THORNE (Beehives) LTD

BEEHIVE WORKS • WRAGBY • MARKET RASEN • LINCS • LN8 5LA

Directors:
P. B. SMITH
G. SMITH
L. L. THORNE
J. THORNE

Beekeeping & Candlemaking Equipment Manufacturers

13th July 1999

Mr R. Cooper
Brondesbury Villas
London

Dear Mr Cooper

Thank you for your letter of July 12th concerning 'Waspard'. Very
interesting, but do not associate our name with the product.

Yours sincerely

P.B. Smith
Managing Director

END OF CORRESPONDENCE

Mr D P Cody
Aluminium Foil Container Manufacturers' Association
Wickfield House
Disney Place
London

22nd July 1999

Dear Mr Cody,

How are you? I'm fine.

I'll get to the point. I am a young poet in need of sponsoring. Would your organisation sponsor me?

Here's a poem I wrote all about the Aluminium Foil Container Manufacturers' Association. It's actually a song to be sung to the tune of 'O My Darling Clementine':

> O my darling,
> O my darling,
> O my darling tell the nation
> It's the Aluminium, Foil Container
> Manufacturers' Association
>
> They work so late,
> They work so hard,
> From their special condominium,
> Representing different companies,
> That use aluminium
>
> They're so friendly,
> They're so clever,
> They can make things with their hands,
> Like little boxes made of metal
> Just to keep your rubber bands
>
> So let's sing loud,
> And let's sing proud,
> For the AFCMA
> Let's hope that they continue,
> ?????????????????????????????

The last line is missing on purpose. Can you or your employees suggest a good final line? Please write back with your suggestions. Perhaps you could have the poem printed on your company ties. You could charge, say, 3 quid a tie and I could get 30p commission. What do you reckon?

Yours sincerely,

Robin Coop

Robin Cooper

NO RESPONSE

41

Robin Cooper
Brondesbury Villas
London

Mike Ring
British Egg Association
Suite 101
Albany House
324-326 Regent Street
W1R 5AA

22nd July 1999

Dear Mr Mike Ring,

My Spirit Guide, Mr Krisp (a yellow ant), is convinced that Hollywood actor Tom Selleck is the honorary Chairman of the British Egg Association.

I scoffed at the suggestion, but Mr Krisp is adam-ant. He also assured me that several of his co-worker ants have seen Mr Selleck's face printed on various egg cartons.

Is this true? Can I phone The Sun if it is?

Please write back to me ASAP.

Yours sincerely,

Robin Cooper

Cc Mr Krisp

The British Egg Association

Secretary: Miss Louisa Platt

Suite 101
Albany House
234 - 326 regent Street
London W1R 5AA

Robin Cooper
Brondesbury Villas
London

23 August 1999

Dear Mr Robin Cooper,

Thank you for your letter of 22nd July 1999.

For your information, the Chairman of the BEA is Mr Andrew Jorêt. I have also enclosed one of our leaflets for you............ not a famous face in sight!

Yours Sincerely,

Louisa Platt

Association Secretary

END OF CORRESPONDENCE

Robin Cooper
Brondesbury Villas
London

G R Wanstall
Campaign for National Service
Lancaster Road
Wincheap
Canterbury Kent

18th August 1999

Dear Mr Wanstall,

First of all let me begin my letter herein in a congratulatory manner. I should like to say "well done" for all your excellent work. I too am a staunch (firm) believer in National Service and feel that had this country had it, then it had better been better to live in – in every respect!

I will now get round to the point of my letter…

I have a young daughter named Lisa. I say young because she's 9. Of late, Lisa has been behaving rather unrulally. Below is a list of her discretions:

1)   Leaving her room in a mess.
2)   Answering back to her mother (who has a bad ankle).
3)   Using far too much washing-up liquid when washing up. One only needs a tiny bit as it is in concentrated form.
4)   Losing three buttons from her jacket last Sunday.
5)   Failing to make sufficiently 'fluffy' meringues.

I feel the only solution is for my daughter to be enrolled – at once – into the armed forces, possibly within a fighting unit. I really believe that this will make her realise the error of her ways.

Could you please write back, enclosing an official form with details of her barracks etc.

Many thanks in advance and may you continue with your fabulous work.

Yours sincerely,

[signature: R. Cooper]

Robin Cooper

R/C
20-8-99 Reply

A NOTE (in haste)

I return your letter as it is so very silly! A lack of regard for good citizenship is everywhere – the next time you are troubled with "yobs" think of this!! I don't think your child needs my assistance – but clearly a person who behaves so stupidly could indeed benefit from improved citizenship and common sense! G. R. Wanstall.

END OF CORRESPONDENCE

* I return your letter as it is so very silly! A lack of regard for good citizenship is everywhere – the next time you are troubled with 'yobs' think of this!! I don't think your child needs my assistance – but clearly a person who behaves so stupidly could indeed benefit from improved citizenship and common sense! G R Wanstall

44

Robin Cooper
Brondesbury Villas
London

Stella Nicholas
Honorary Secretary
The United Kingdom Spoon Collectors Club
High Street
West Molesey
Surrey

25th August 1999

Dear Stella,

- Hello, come in. Would you like a cup of tea?

- Yes please. Thank you.

- Sugar?

- Please. My, what a fine spoon.

- I thank you. For I am a collector (of spoons).

An everyday scene from within my home. No doubt yours too.

Please excuse my impudence. I am Robin Cooper and I have one of the largest collections of spoons in Britain.

I am now ready to open my hitherto secret passion up to the public, and would be most grateful if you could please advise me as to the best way to present these wonderful spoons, (11,000 at the last count) to the soon-to-be-bewildered-but-amazed masses?

I look forward to hearing from you.

Keep up all the great work.

Best wishes,

Robin Cooper

UNITED KINGDOM SPOON COLLECTORS CLUB

Please reply to:
Mrs Stella Nicholas
High Street
West Molesey
Surrey

Dear Robin,

Thank you for your letter telling me about your amazing spoon collection. Where do you keep them all? I think the largest collection held by one of our members is 3,500 but Des Warren in Australia has over 30,000!!

He has built an annex to his house so that the public can see his spoons and raises money for charity.

We only show spoons on a very small scale in comparison and find that tiny dots of velcro work very well at holding the standard sizes spoons in position. Apart from that I do not have very much advice to give.

I enclose some details about our club and wish you all the best in your undertaking – do let us know if you get the project off the ground and we will come and see the presentation.

Yours sincerely

Stella Nicholas

Stella Nicholas
Hon Secretary

END OF CORRESPONDENCE

Robin Cooper
Brondesbury Villas
London

Mr Jeremy Collins
The Miniaturists' Trade Association
c/o Gable End Designs
Station Road
Knowle
Solihull

25th August 1999

Dear Mr Collins,

A friend of mine (I cannot divulge his/her name for fear of reprisals) mentioned to me your organisation, The Miniaturists' Trade Association.

Apparently, and correct me if I (or he/she) am (is) wrong, you represent manufacturers of dolls, doll's houses and associated miniatures.

Well, I have been designing doll's houses since the year dot (1989) and they really are very good. I work chiefly in paper and chicken bone, weaving the two materials together into lattice-like structures. The doll's houses are then assembled by children who are paid approx. 40p an hour.

Can I send you some of my sketches? I would really like to become a fully-fledged member of your association. I promise I'll behave.

Many, many thanks.

I anticipate your response with gusto,

Yours sincerely,

Robin Cooper

Robin Cooper

MINIATURISTS' TRADE ASSOCIATION

Patron: Vivien M. Greene   •   President : David Kilpatrick

Mr Robin Cooper
Brondesbury Villas
London

Please reply to: Jeremy Collins
Buckland Newton
Nr Dorchester
Dorset

1 September 1999

Our Ref: JSC/388.ENQ

Dear Mr Cooper,

Thank you for your enquiry about MinTA, the Miniaturists' Trade Association. As the UK's only Trade Association devoted entirely to miniaturists, we currently have a membership of around 120 craftspeople and organisations, drawn from all disciplines of the industry. Membership of MinTA is open to all who are active on a commercial basis in the Miniatures business, subject to the approval of the National Committee.

I enclose some information about MinTA and a Membership Application Form.

However, I have to advise you that I do not think the Committee would countenance approving membership for an organisation employing child labour.

Yours sincerely,

Jeremy Collins

Jeremy Collins, Coordinator

END OF CORRESPONDENCE

Mr C S Reynolds
Director
The Freshwater Biological Association
The Ferry House
Far Sawrey
Ambleside
Cumbria
LA22 0LP

27th August 1999

Dear Mr Reynolds,

As far as I understand, your association investigates the biology of animals and plants found in fresh and brackish water.

Well, I have something that I'm sure you'll be interested in.

I have a small pond in my back garden. It has been rather neglected as of late (I've been very busy fixing my wretched shed) but it does contain some fish. Anyway, I was removing some old clothes from the bottom of the pond the other day, when I saw the strangest looking fish/amphibian/bird creature I have ever seen. It really has to be seen to be believed.

I am convinced that this is an entirely new species.

I have made some detailed sketches of this 'freak of nature'. Would you like me to send you my drawings?

I await your reply.

Kindest regards,

Robin Cooper

49

FRESHWATER BIOLOGICAL ASSOCIATION

A Company Limited by Guarantee
Registered No. 263162, England

Registered Charity No. 214440

The Ferry House
Far Sawrey
AMBLESIDE
Cumbria LA22 0LP

Robin Cooper
Brondesbury Villas
London

Chief Executive
Dr Roger Sweeting FIFM

RS/SG

7 September, 1999

Dear Mr Cooper

Thank you for your most intriguing letter describing your strange-looking creature. We would be only too pleased to see photographs – perhaps we might be able to assist you in its identification.

Yours sincerely

Dr Roger Sweeting

Robin Cooper
Brondesbury Villas
London

Dr Roger Sweeting
Chief Executive
The Freshwater Biological Association
The Ferry House
Far Sawrey
Ambleside
Cumbria
LA22 0LP

12th September 1999

Dear Dr Sweeting,

Many thanks for your letter regarding my 'strange-looking creature' that has been lurking in and around my pond.

I do not have any photos as I do not have a camera. However, as I mentioned in my first letter, I have made some sketches of the beast.

I enclose one of these (sketches), and would be very keen for you to tell me just what species it is.

I should also like to know whether we should try to destroy this being. My wife is very scared of it and keeps begging me to pour bleach into the pond. Is this wise?

I look forward to your help.

Kindest regards,

Robin Cooper

Strange Creature in My Pond
(Size: 8 inches high)

Tentacles

Wings

Beak

Tail

Little claws on feet

Leaves (source of food)

END OF CORRESPONDENCE

Robin Cooper
Brondesbury Villas
London

Stephen Bennett
Honorary Secretary
The Clarinet Heritage Society
Hambalt Road
London

28th August 1999

Dear Bennett (Mr),

I am a keen lover of all things clarinettal. The lull of reed against palette, the rasp of tongue against mouthpiece are somethings I have always cherished. You are a lucky man, Bennett, working amongst such fine instruments. In some ways I envy you.

The reason for my writing of this letter is that I am trying to organise a surprise birthday party for my wife. I will hold it at home, on October 9th. This is not the actual date of my wife's birthday, so it will be a double surprise!

I aim to gather 200 clarinettists together inside my house. As soon as my wife comes home from work, the clarinettists take out their instruments and get ready to play. My wife will no doubt be incredibly surprised. But wait, Bennett, the clarinettists do not play a single note. They simply lay down their instruments and file silently out of the house.

She certainly won't expect that!

I would be grateful if you could help me find 200 professional clarinettists. It is vital that each and everyone is of concert standard.

I look forward to your reply and thank you, in anticipation, for your hard work.

Best wishes,

Robin Cooper

Robin Cooper

31 August 1999

Dear Mr. Cooper

Thank you for your intriguing letter.

There are indeed more than 200 professional clarinettists of "concert standard" abounding.

Pond life being as it is, clarinettists are forever being exploited by the profession constantly. The problem here is how to persuade 200 of them to participate.

I would need to know more about your surprise party for your wife. What can I say to these clars. to partake of this plan?

I look forward to hearing from you.

Yours sincerely,

Stephen Bennett

47 Hambalt Road
Clapham
London SW4 9EQ
England
Tel: (81) 675 3877

Robin Cooper
Brondesbury Villas
London

Stephen Bennett
Honorary Secretary
The Clarinet Heritage Society
Hambalt Road
London

2nd September 1999

Dear Bennett (Mr),

Thank you ever so much for such a speedy reply to my letter. I thank you, Bennett, it was greatly appreciated. Incidentally, I did like the pen you used – it really showed off all the 'flourishes'. Where did you get it?

I am glad you think that the surprise party for my wife would be a good idea and pleased to hear you're on board.

You requested some more info regarding the event so that you could forward it to the 200 clarinettists (or 'clars' as you describe them).

I would like the clarinettists to arrive at 6:00pm sharp. They will then be told to take up positions. I would like 40 to be in the hallway, 36 on the stairs (2 per step), 20 in the kitchen, 30 in the living room, 40 on the first floor landing, and 34 in my daughter's bedroom.

My wife should be arriving home at 6:30pm. As soon as she walks through the door, the clarinettists are to do what was laid out in my previous letter

"...the clarinettists take out their instruments and get ready to play. My wife will no doubt be incredibly surprised. But wait, Bennett, the clarinettists do not play a single note. They simply lay down their instruments and file silently out of the house..."

Refreshments will be provided.

Is this enough info? What else would you need to know to make this an evening of a lifetime?

I look forward to your reply. I thank you again with all my heart.

Best wishes,

Robin Cooper

END OF CORRESPONDENCE

Robin Cooper
Brondesbury Villas
London

Dr George Carey
The Archbishop of Canterbury
Lambeth Palace
London
SE1 7JU

31st August 1999

Dear Archbishop,

I hope you are very well.

I am writing to you for your learned advice.

I am thinking of starting up my own religion. Unfortunately I'm a bit stuck on a number of issues, such as what we should believe in, how we pray, what to call ourselves etc.

As a religious man could you perhaps give me a few tips as to the best way to set up an entirely new world religion.

I look forward to your response.

Best wishes,

Yours sincerely,

Robin Cooper

LAMBETH PALACE

Robin Cooper Esq
Brondesbury Villas
London

Public Affairs Office
Louis Henderson

2 September 1999

Dear Mr Cooper,

I have been asked by the Archbishop of Canterbury to thank you for your recent letter, the contents of which have been noted.

I am sure that you will not be surprised that Dr Carey is unable to advise you on how to found your own religion. If in approaching him you are seeking the help of the Church of England to meet your immediate spiritual needs, the Archbishop would advise you to approach your own local clergy, or other Christians in whom you have confidence.

Yours sincerely,

LOUIS HENDERSON

END OF CORRESPONDENCE

Lambeth Palace, London SE1 7JU

Dr Frank Hauxwell
British Colour Maker's Association
37 St George's Square
Chadderton
Oldham
Lancs. OL9 9NY

10th July 1999

Dear Dr Frank Hauxwell,

Fanfare please!

I think you'd better enrol me as a new member, for I have invented a new colour.

It's not a shade, or a hue, or even a tinge. No, it's a simple, pure, unique colour. I call it Greem.

I have no words to describe greem, as that would involve mentioning other colours that might look a bit like it, and since there aren't any, I can't.

But I will try...

Greem is like a field of undiluted emotion, cut clean with steel scissors, wielded by a fragrant farmgirl who has just written a 'Belated Happy Birthday' card to her dearest nephew.

I hope this gives you a clearer picture of what greem looks like, but if you would like to see a sample of my new colour, please write back – enclosing my membership card to your organisation.

I look forward to hearing from you.

Kind wishes,

Robin Cooper

Robin Cooper

BRITISH COLOUR MAKERS ASSOCIATION

37 ST GEORGES SQUARE • CHADDERTON • OLDHAM • OL9 9NY • UK

SECRETARY: Dr FRANK HAUXWELL

Robin Cooper
Brondesbury Villas
London

6 September, 1999

Dear Mr Cooper,

Ref. "Green"

Thank you for your correspondence on "Green" ; my apologies for not replying sooner.

BCMA is a Trade Association for manufactures of pigments, operating in the United Kingdom, Membership is not available to individuals.

If you wish to discuss the development of your ideas, I would be happy to put you in touch with one or more of our members.

To do this effectively, I would ask that you forward to me any information, demonstration panels, patent information or samples which you have and which you are willing to make available.

Yours sincerely,

Frank Hauxwell.

Robin Cooper
Brondesbury Villas
London

Dr Frank Hauxwell
British Colour Maker's Association
37 St George's Square
Chadderton
Oldham
Lancs. OL9 9NY

10th September 1999

Dear Dr Frank Hauxwell,

Thank you for your letter of reply that you sent to me.

If you cast your mind backwards a little, you will recall that I have invented a new, individually unique colour. It is called Greem.

You asked me to send you a sample. Unfortunately, at present I am unable to do this. As you will probably appreciate, I do have to be careful about sending out a sample of a potentially lucrative colour. I trust that you are not offended.

However, I have a solution.

I will travel up to Oldham on the weekend of the 27th September. I will paint a 6 inch stripe of Greem paint on the Mumps bridge, just off the A62 Oldham Road. As you know, this is an iron bridge, and you will find my sample painted on the 26th railing along from the left. You will then be free to view my colour at your leisure.

I hope that this is a satisfactory arrangement. Please do get back to me ASAP so that I can arrange my train tickets.

Many thanks,

Yours sincerely,

Robin Cooper

Robin Cooper
Brondesbury Villas
London

September 15, 1999

Dear Mr Cooper,

Your letter of the 10th September is noted.

The Association could not condone the action which you propose, which could be viewed as an act of Criminal Damage on private property.

Please do not send any further correspondence on this subject to the Association.

Yours sincerely,

Frank Hauxwell.

END OF CORRESPONDENCE

Robin Cooper
Brondesbury Villas
London

Mikael Ohlsson
Managing Director
IKEA Sweden AB
Pulpanvagen
Box 702 S34381
Almhult
Sweden

31st August 1999

Dear Mikael,

I am a young - well, youngish - furniture designer. I have won many competitions and my work has filled the homes of such well-known figures as Brian Furbish and Katie Billingham (to name just two!).

For the past three years I have been working on a new range of bedroom furniture. I have just finished the designs and have been told that they are perfect for IKEA.

Can I send you the designs? I just know you're gonna love them.

I await your reply.

Keep up all the wonderful work,

Best wishes,

Robin Cooper

PS – My son also shares your name, although it is spelt with a 'ch' rather than a 'k'.

IKEA of Sweden AB

1999-09-09
Robin Cooper
Brondesbury Villas
London
UK

Date/Datum

Your date/Er datum

Our reference/Vår referens

Your reference/Er referens

Dear Mr Cooper,

As you understand it is difficult for us to decide if we are interested or not of your product before knowing more about it.
The best and easiest way for both parts, is if you can send us a photo or a sketch or an other description of the product you think fit into IKEAs range. We have a large range and get a lot of suggestions of cooperation. Our Product responsible need to know more about the product before they arrange a meeting with the designer.

I will also explain what policy apply for external suggestions. IKEA never pay royalty. If we are interested we begin an negotiation where IKEA at the price agreed take over all rights to produce and sell the product in question.

The usual procedure for this is that a sketch, photo or some other documentation is sent to us together with a presentation by the designer. The letter is then forwarded to the Product Manager responsible for the product area to which the product would belong. He/She estimantes whether the product is of any interest to IKEA.

IKEAs principal is that we do not sign any kind of secrecy agreement. The reason of that is that we never can guarantee that IKEA are doing the same kind of product at the same time.
What we however can guarantee is that we are not attend to steal your idéa, if and now you are showing your product for us.
If you anyway hesitate to show your product I suggest you to legal protect it before.

If the idea, for any reason, is not considered to suit our range, the material sent to IKEA is returned to the designer.

The address is: IKEA of Sweden AB
                    Design dep.
                    Box 702
                    343 81 Älmhult
                    Sweden

Once again thanks for contacting us.

Yours sincerely,

IKEA of Sweden AB
Design dep.

Maria Ohlsson

Postadress/Postal address	Org nr/Org. No.	Telefon/Telephone	Telex	Telefax	Bank	Postgiro account	Bankgiro account
IKEA of Sweden AB	556074-7551	Nat 0476-810 00		Nat 0476-127 17			
Box 702		Int. +46 476-810 00	52034	Int. +46 476-127 17			
S-343 81 ALMHULT							
SWEDEN							

Robin Cooper
Brondesbury Villas
London

Maria Ohlsson
Managing Director
IKEA Sweden AB
Pulpanvagen
Box 702 S34381
Almhult
Sweden

20th September 1999

Our (your) reference/Var referens

Your (my) reference/Er referens

Dear Maria,

Thank you for your letter of the 9th September. I must apologise for calling you 'Mikael' in my previous correspondence. There is no excuse. I must be punished.

Anyway, if you remember, I am a youngish furniture designer and have just completed a new range of stuff for the bedroom that is absolutely IDEAL for IKEA.

You asked me to send you some sketches, so please find enclosed a drawing for my TIMPAARSYAM BED/SHELF UNIT. It is both fire and water proof.

I hope you enjoy my designs and look forward to your company putting my ideas into production.

Keep up the fabulous work.

Best wishes,

R. Li Coq

Robin Cooper

TIMPAARSYAM BED/SHELF UNIT. (SELF-ASSEMBLY)

DESIGN BY ROBIN COOPER.

PRICE £ 89.99

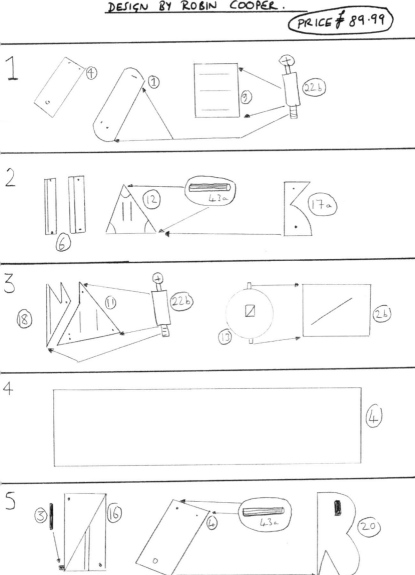

Mr Robin Cooper
Brondesbury Villas
London   Älmhult November 29, 1999

Hello,

I work as a productdeveloper at IKEA of Sweden, IKEA's
range & supply company.

I have received your letter addressed to Maria Ohlsson in which you
describe a possible product for IKEA.

We have a number of small shelves in our range today and at the moment
we do not plan to increase articles in this businessarea.

Thank you for showing interest and enclosed you will find your
sketch.

Best regards,

Tomas Lundin
IKEA of Sweden
Box 702
S-343 81 Älmhult
Sweden

END OF CORRESPONDENCE

Robin Cooper
Brondesbury Villas
London

Charles Kennedy
The Leader of the Liberal Democrat Party
House of Commons
Westminster
London
SW1A 2PW

31st August 1999

Dear Mr Kennedy,

You're the man!

I'm writing to you as a keen supporter (of what you do and also stand for).

Let me introduce myself. I am Robin Cooper, designer. I have designed a range of logos which I feel would be perfect for your party. Would you be so kind as to allow me to send them to you?

I look forward to hearing from you, Sir.

Kind regards,

R. L. Cooper

Robin Cooper

HOUSE OF COMMONS
LONDON SW1A 0AA

Mr Robin Cooper
Brondesbury Villas
LONDON

13 September, 1999
Our Reference: nh/ijp/ack

Dear Mr Cooper

Thank you for your recent letter and your kind congratulations.

I am grateful to you for writing to me on this issue. However, the issue of the party logo really falls under the responsibility of Kate Fox, Communications Officer for the Liberal Democrats and I have therefore copied your letter on to her, for her information.

Thank you once again for writing.

Yours sincerely,

Charles Kennedy MP
(Dictated by Mr Kennedy and signed in his absence)

cc Kate Fox

Liberal Democrats

Party Headquarters
4 Cowley Street
London SW1P 3NB

Telephone   0171 222 7999
Fax   0171 799 2170

Mr Robin Cooper
Brondesbury Villas
London

29th September 1999

Dear Mr Cooper,

I am writing to you with reference to your letter to Charles Kennedy MP dated 31st August 1999. As you know, Charles Kennedy's office passed your letter on to me.

The Liberal Democrats have just launched a new revised logo which was designed by Rodney Fitch Design Company. Fitch designed the original Bird of Liberty and have subsequently made an evolutionary rather than revolutionary change to the bird.

We are using up our old stocks of stationery before using the new logo which is why the new design does not feature on this letter. However, do feel free to contact me if you would like to see the new design.

If you would still like to send me copies of your designs I would be more than happy to look at them. I will file your letter and any designs that you send for future reference.

Many thanks for your very kind offer.

Yours sincerely,

Kate Fox
Communications Officer

Robin Cooper
Brondesbury Villas
London

Kate Fox
Communications Officer
The Liberal Democrat Party
House of Commons
Westminster
London
SW1A 2PW

31st September 1999

Dear Kate,

Many thanks for your letter of 29th September that acted as a replyal to mine sent on 31st August.

If you recall, I am a designer and have a number of logos that I feel would suit your party (the Lib Dems).

You did indeed request a perusal of the said items, and I hereby enclose them herewith. The designs are based on the five senses – touch, sight, hearing, smell and tasting.

I welcome your thoughts, and hopefully you will pass them on to Mr Kennedy himself for his own personal judgement.

I await your reply.

Kind regards,

R. Li Coo

Robin Cooper

DESIGNS FOR A SET OF NEW LOGOS
FOR CHARLES KENNEDY'S LIBERAL DEMOCRATS

TOUCH

moth

SIGHT

Moth

HEARING

moth ear

SMELL

moth

TASTING

Crab

moth 'eaten'

Robin Cooper

Liberal Democrats

Party Headquarters
4 Cowley Street
London SW1P 3NB

Telephone   0171 222 7999
Fax   0171 799 2170

Mr Robin Cooper
Brondesbury Villas
London

7th October 1999

Dear Mr Cooper,

LIBERAL DEMOCRAT PARTY LOGO

Many thanks for your letter of 31st September and for your logo designs which are most interesting.

As the party logo has just been re-designed, there will not be a further change of this kind for ma years let alone any consultation on this matter.

However, I have filed your letter and designs for future reference.

With kind regards,

Kate Fox
Communications Officer

END OF CORRESPONDENCE

Robin Cooper
Brondesbury Villas
London

Dawn Doory
Customer Services Manager
Next Plc
Desford Road
Enderby
Leicester
LE9 5AT

1st September 1999

Dear Dawn,

My son's birthday is fast approaching but I am at a loss as to what to buy him. I have decided that it is time Michael got himself a new wardrobe, but being his father I know I'll only go out and buy all the wrong clothes! (Hats, gloves and countless silly scarves!!!!!!)

Rather than me spending lots of money on clothes that he will only throw in the bin or, even worse, burn, I think it's best for me to buy some of your gift vouchers. That way Michael can choose whatever takes his fancy.

Could you please tell me how I would arrange to purchase £10,000 worth of Next vouchers?

I look forward to hearing from you.

Yours sincerely,

Robin Cooper

CUSTOMER SERVICE DEPT, DESFORD ROAD, ENDERBY, LEICESTER, LE9 5AT
TELEPHONE 0870 243 5435 - FAX 0116 284 2318
E MAIL Enquiries@next.co.uk

Our Ref: 935186/RD
6 September 1999

Mr Robin Cooper
Brondesbury Villas
London

Dear Mr Cooper,

Thank you for your recent letter.

May I firstly say how pleased I am that you and your son have chosen to shop with our Company.

We would be more than happy to sell you £10,000 of gift vouchers. I would advise however, that Next gift vouchers do have an expiry date and remaining vouchers would need to be replaced annually. Also, lost or stolen vouchers cannot be cancelled and therefore, cannot be replaced. Therefore, for reasons of practicality, we would actually recommend a Next Store Card with the money credited to it.

We would be able to offer 5% discount on the money credited to the Store card, or 2½% discount should you decide to purchase the gift vouchers.

If you should find the Store Card option acceptable, then please contact Tracy Duddle, Administration Manager at the Next Directory, whereby the arrangements for payment etc, will be explained.

If however, you still wish to purchase the gift vouchers or have any further enquiries, please feel free to contact myself at the above address where I will endeavour to assist in any way I can.

Yours sincerely

Dawn Doory
<u>Customer Service Manager</u>

NEXT RETAIL LTD, DESFORD ROAD, ENDERBY, LEICESTER LE9 5AT. TELEPHONE 0116-286 6411
TELEX 34415 NEXT G. FACSIMILE 0116-284 8998.

REGISTERED IN ENGLAND 123434, REGISTERED OFFICE, DESFORD ROAD, ENDERBY, LEICESTER LE9 5AT.

0104

Robin Cooper
Brondesbury Villas
London

Dawn Doory
Customer Services Manager
Next Plc
Desford Road
Enderby
Leicester
LE9 5AT

17th September 1999

Our (your) Ref: 935186/RD

Dear Dawn,

Many thanks for your letter of 6th September, replying to mine of 1st September.

I was rather confused when I read your note, and I quote:

"We (you) would be more than happy to sell you (me) £10,000 of gift vouchers".

Ten thousand pounds?! Ten THOUSAND pounds?! TEN thousand pounds?!
Ten thousand POUNDS?! Do you think I'm made of money?!!

I wrote to you asking how I would purchase £10 of vouchers – ten pounds, not ten thousand pounds.

I can only assume that you have made a typing error. I do forgive you. We all make mistakes – not even I.

Please could you therefore advise me on how to purchase ten pounds (£10) of gift vouchers for my son, Michael.

I look forward to hearing from you again and keep up all the fabulous work at Next Clothes.

Yours sincerely,

Robin Cooper

NEXT

CUSTOMER SERVICE DEPT, DESFORD ROAD, ENDERBY, LEICESTER, LE9 5AT
TELEPHONE 0870 243 5435 - FAX 0116 284 2318
E MAIL Enquiries@next.co.uk

Our Ref: 935186a/SH
20 September 1999

Mr Robin Cooper
Brondesbury Villas
London

Dear Mr Cooper,

Thank you for your most recent letter and I was sorry to learn of the confusion you felt when reading our response to your gift voucher enquiry.

At Next we do aim to ensure that our letters are as accurate as possible and take into account all the points raised by the customer. As you can see from the enclosed copy, your letter did state that you wanted to purchase £10,000 worth of gift vouchers. However, it would appear that this was an error and I can fully appreciate the surprise and confusion you must have felt when reading our reply.

Fortunately, purchasing £10.00 worth of vouchers is far less complicated than purchasing £10,000 worth. Our vouchers are available from any Next store.

Thank you for taking the time and trouble to contact us about this matter and I hope you will remain a much valued customer of Next.

Yours sincerely,

Dawn Doory
Customer Service Manager

END OF CORRESPONDENCE

NEXT RETAIL LTD, DESFORD ROAD, ENDERBY, LEICESTER LE9 5AT. TELEPHONE 0116-286 6411 FAX 0116-284 8998.
CUSTOMER SERVICES TELEPHONE 08702 435435

REGISTERED IN ENGLAND 123434, REGISTERED OFFICE, DESFORD ROAD, ENDERBY, LEICESTER LE9 5AT

0140

Robin Cooper
Brondesbury Villas
London

Ernesto Spinelli
Society of Existential Analysis
BM Existential
London WC1N 3XX

15th December 1999

Dear Mr Spinelli,

Why did I choose to write this letter?

Yours sincerely,

Robin Cooper

**School of
Psychotherapy
and Counselling**

Regent's College
Inner Circle
Regent's Park
London NW1 4NS
UK

10th January 2000

Robin Cooper
Brondesbury Villas
LONDON

Dear Robin Cooper

"You are not the Do-er." (Gautama Buddha)

By the way, *what* letter?

END OF CORRESPONDENCE

Yours sincerely

Professor Ernesto Spinelli

77

Robin Cooper
Brondesbury Villas
London

Lesley Munro-Faure
The National Society for Quality Through Teamwork
Castle Street
Salisbury
Wilts.

29th February 2000

Dear Mr Munro-Faure,

Allow me to introduce myself. I am Robin Cooper. Lizard breeder.

I have been breeding and studying lizards for the past 12 years. Through my research I have found that these wonderful creatures are, in fact, excellent team players. They respond well to instruction, and with persistence, can be fully trained within about three months.

I have successfully trained a group of 12 lizards in the game of Tug-Of-War. A small piece of string or gauze is gripped by both teams of lizards who attempt, upon my whistle, to drag their opposing team over the line (usually marked out by chalk).

I think you'll agree that this is an amazing example of the benefits of teamwork, and I have been giving talks about my lizards and their teamwork abilities throughout the Southeast.

Here's where you can help (hopefully!): I'm currently preparing a 'Lizard Tug-Of-War Roadshow'. This involves travelling with both teams of lizards up and down the country, and putting on shows that demonstrate the art of reptile teamwork. Since I am in need of financial assistance, I wonder if your organisation – The National Society for Quality Through Teamwork – would be interested in sponsoring me. In return I will paint your organisation's logo onto the backs of all team members.

I look forward to hearing from you.

Best wishes,

Robin Cooper

Robin Cooper

Castle Street
Salisbury

National Society for Quality through Teamwork

23rd March 2000

Robin Cooper
Brondesbury Villas
London

Dear Mr Cooper

Many thanks for your recent letters. I am sorry for the delay in responding but I wanted to explore the opportunity with our management committee before replying.

Unfortunately we do not feel that we are able to sponsor your road show at the present time since we already have a number of other commitments. May I take the opportunity to wish you all the best with your venture – we would like to hear how you get on and may be able to feature your road show in a future edition of our newsletter should you have an appropriate write-up/photos etc.

Yours sincerely

Lesley Munro-Faure
Executive Director

END OF CORRESPONDENCE

Robin Cooper
Brondesbury Villas
London

Mr J Connell
Chairman
The Noise Abatement Society
PO Box 518
Eynsford
Dartford
Kent
DA4 0LL

16th March 2000

Dear Mr Connell,

Greetings from one noise disliker to another!

I too feel that noise, or over-excessive volume, is an affront to our senses. In fact, it is nothing but ear filth, which must be destroyed.

That is where I come in. I am an inventor of electrical devices. For the past 9 years I have been developing a machine which, when placed in a room, can reduce all aggravating sounds by a factor of twenty-five.

I am now ready to unveil the machine, which I have christened **The Imsimil-Berati-Lahn**. The machine is cheap, durable and 100% effective. I have already tested it on national radio with amazing results. A spot on BBC's 'Tomorrow's World' is in the pipeline.

Would your organization be interested in receiving a sneak preview of **The Imsimil-Berati-Lahn**? I can provide diagrams and full explanations of its workings.

I look forward to hearing from you – keep up the good work.

Best wishes,

Robin Cooper

P.O. BOX NO. 518, EYNSFORD, DARTFORD, KENT DA4 0LL.

noise abatement society

Founded July 1959   Registered Charity No. 272040

founder & chairman:
JOHN CONNELL, OBE FIEnvSc MIPR
vice chairman:
HARRY KENYON, BSc,MIMechE,CEng. MIOA

Mr Robin Cooper
Brondesbury Villas
LONDON

20.4.00

Dear Mr Cooper

The Imsimil- Berati -Lahn

Thankyou for your recent letter regarding your machine for reducing sound and we apologise for the belated reply.

We have consulted with our acoustic engineer , he is very interested and would like to have further details of the machine. We look forward to hearing from you in the near future.

Yours sincerely

S. Boswell
pp. T.ADLER

Robin Cooper
Brondesbury Villas
London

Mr S Boswell
pp T. Adler
The Noise Abatement Society
PO Box 518
Eynsford
Dartford
Kent
DA4 0LL

25th May 2000

Dear Mr Boswell,

Many thanks for your letter of reply dated 20th April. Please accept my sincere apologies for the delay (in response). My wife and I have been in Bruges for the past few weeks due to my emphysema.

If you recall, I have designed a machine, **The Imsimil-Berati-Lahn**, which can reduce noisy sounds by a factor of twenty-five. I was delighted to learn that your acoustic engineer was intereste in it and requested some more info. I enclose a diagram of the device, which I trust will throw some more light on the **The Imsimil-Berati-Lahn**'s workings.

What's the next step? I would obviously be interested in mass-producing **The Imsimil-Berati-Lahns** for the mass markets (the EU, Asia/Pacific etc.).

I look forward to hearing from you.

Keep up the good work.

Best wishes,

Robin Cooper

82

THE IMSIMIL-BERATI-LAHN

'NOISE REDUCTION BY A 25 FACTOR'
DESIGN BY ROBIN COOPER

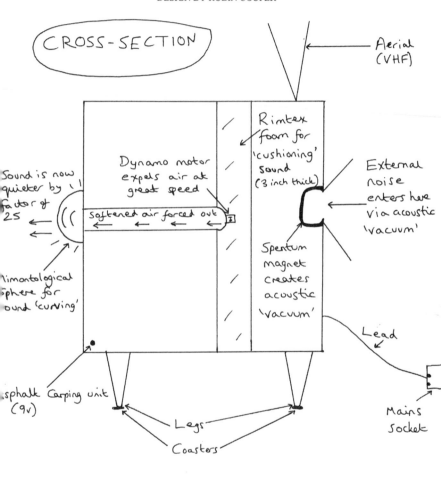

CROSS-SECTION

Aerial (VHF)

Rimtex foam for 'cushioning' sound (3 inch thick)

Dynamo motor expels air at great speed

Sound is now quieter by a factor of 25

Softened air forced out

External noise enters here via acoustic 'vacuum'

Spentum magnet creates acoustic 'vacuum'

Mimontological sphere for sound 'curving'

Lead

Asphalk Carping unit (9v)

Legs

Coasters

Mains Socket

© Robin Cooper, 2000

Actual size

P.O. BOX NO. 518, EYNSFORD, DARTFORD, KENT DA4 0LL.

noise abatement society

Founded July 1959   Registered Charity No. 27204

founder & chairman:
JOHN CONNELL, OBE FIEnvSc MIPR
vice chairman:
HARRY KENYON, BSc,MIMechE,CEng. MIOA

Robin Cooper
Brondesbury Villas
London

17th July 2000

Dear Mr Cooper

Thank you for your recent communication, as you know we have forwarded your drawing to
our consultants , and we wish you well in the further development of your design and hope
that you find a market for the idea.

Yours sincerely

pp.
T. Adler
Hon Secretary

END OF CORRESPONDENCE

Robin Cooper
Brondesbury Villas
London

Mr P Hutton
Chairman
The Ronald Stevenson Society
Chamberlain Road
Edinburgh

16th March 2000

Dear Mr Hutton,

I was flicking through a telephone directory the other day when I came across your organisation, 'The Ronald Stevenson Society'.

Have I gone mad? I went to the same school as Ronald Stevenson thirty odd years ago. In fact, I was even in the same class. As far as I can recall, Ronald was a deeply unpopular boy. He had no friends to speak of, would regularly burst into tears for no apparent reason, and once drank an entire beaker of horse and pig excrement as a bet (for which he was caned). His nickname was 'Stinkapple Stevenson'.

How on earth has Ronald Stevenson managed to set up his own fan club? I can only assume he has totally changed. Perhaps he has found God. Or started washing.

Could you please enlighten me.

I look forward to hearing from you.

Yours sincerely,

Robin Cooper

High Street
Peebles
24 March 2000

Dear Mr Cooper,

Our Ronald Stevenson is a distinguished musician, a composer pianist and scholar, and has no connection with the person of the same name known to you.

Yours sincerely,

Philip Hutton

END OF CORRESPONDENCE

Robin Cooper
Brondesbury Villas
London

Norma Curtis
Honorary Secretary
The Romantic Novelists' Association
Makepeace Ave
London

16th March 2000

Dear Norma

I have heard about your wonderful association through the well-known romantic novelist, Dr Jeremy Fulvere, (author of 'Dr Cannon's Love', 'Dr Hellbridge's Love', 'Dr Samson's Love' and many more).

I have for many years harboured the desire to become a world-ranking novelist. Nothing gives me greater pleasure than to write down scenes about romance on to paper, then imagine they're in some kind of book.

As you're an expert in these things, would you please do me the honour of telling me if I have a chance to become as successful as Dr Fulvere, by reading the following lines of romantic prose, penned by me.

This extract is from my imagined novel entitled, 'He Loved Her':

Mr Limbern loved her. He really did. So much so that it hurt. The tugboat pulled dreamily away from the harbour. Its silky trails were left mid-air, like an interrupted message by some Red Indians.

Sandra looked at him askance.
"I need more time," she said.
"Why?" he asked, distracted by the sound of cork shoes scuffing against the side of the boat.
"Because," she responded, mystically.

The tugboat rounded the corner of the river. A bird – possibly a red turnbill – flew by, its beak carrying a piece of wood and some scrubs for its nest and chicks.

"Look at that," she said. "So free."
"Unlike us," said Mr Limbern. "Unlike us…"

Well, there it is. I would be grateful if you could tell me whether I have a chance to make it in the cut and thrust world of romance. Please be brutal.

Many thanks,

R. Li C.q

Robin Cooper

ROMANTIC NOVELISTS' ASSOCIATION

Makepeace Avenue,
London

R
N
A

22nd March, 2000.

Robin Cooper,
Brondesbury Villas,
London,

Dear Robin,

Many thanks for your lovely letter and sample of prose.

The Romantic Novelists' Association has a New Writer's Scheme for unpublished authors which I am sure you will find helpful. You certainly do have a chance of making it and whether you join or not I think you should carry on being creative, perhaps testing your writing stamina by linking your scenes together coherently until you've made HE LOVED HER into a book.

I am enclosing a membership form. Best wishes to you and good luck with your writing,

Yours sincerely,

Norma Curtis

Norma Curtis
Chairman.

Norma Curtis
Honorary Secretary
The Romantic Novelists' Association
Makepeace Ave
London

27th March 2000

Dear Norma,

Many thanks for your letter of reply to my letter.

I was so delighted when you said, "You (I) certainly do have a chance of making it". It really made my day.

I was also delighted that you enjoyed the sample I sent you from 'He Loved Her', and I have taken your advice to link scenes more coherently. In so doing, I have invented (I hope) an entirely new method of storytelling, designed to 'reach out and touch' the reader. I call this device, the 'Ketwalt Method'.

I have rewritten the same section I sent you, but this time employing the Ketwalt Method:

Mr Limbern loved her. He really did. So much so that it hurt. The tugboat pulled dreamily away from the harbour. Its silky trails were left mid-air, like an interrupted message by some Red Indians. **HELLO READER. PLEASE READ ON…**

Sandra looked at him askance.
"I need more time," she said.
"Why?" he asked, distracted by the sound of cork shoes scuffing against the side of the boat.
"Because," she responded, mystically. **HELLO READER, KEEP READING…**

The tugboat rounded the corner of the river. A bird – possibly a red turnbill – flew by, its beak carrying a piece of wood and some scrubs for its nest and chicks. **ONCE AGAIN, HELLO READER, CONTINUE TO THE NEXT SECTION…**

"Look at that," she said. "So free."
"Unlike us," said Mr Limbern. "Unlike us…" **THANK YOU READER FOR PURSUING WITH MY TEXT. GOD BE WITH YOU.**

Do you feel that I'm onto something? The reason I ask is because I plan to leave my job in two weeks time, as I feel that the Ketwalt Method could be the key to my fortune. However, my wife keeps begging me not to be so "foolish". Could you offer any advice?

Many thanks once again,

Robin Cooper

ROMANTIC NOVELISTS' ASSOCIATION

Makepeace Avenue,
London,

R
N
A

Robin Cooper,
Brondesbury Villas,
London

28th March, 2000.

Dear Robin Cooper,

Thank you for your letter dated 27th March.

I was very interested to read your 'Ketwalt Method' of storytelling.
This idea of bringing the 'author's voice' into the plot has rather gone
out of fashion although it once was very popular. The main drawback of
your new style is that it is rather hectoring and breaks up the narrative
flow.

It's better not to rely on gimmicks - the important thing is to keep
writing and to read over what you've written - revision is the key to
success. Look at publication as a long-term goal and don't give up your
job just yet. John Creasey had 752 rejections before he made it so I'm
siding with your wife on this one.

Very best wishes,

Yours sincerely,

Norma Curtis.

PRESIDENT: DIANE PEARSON

CHAIRMAN: NORMA CURTIS   VICE CHAIRMAN: KATIE FFORDE   SECRETARY: ANNIE MURRAY   TREASURER: KAREN KING

Robin Cooper
Brondesbury Villas
London

Norma Curtis
Honorary Secretary
The Romantic Novelists' Association
Makepeace Ave
London

31st March 2000

Dear Norma,

I would like to thank you for your letter of 28th March 2000. I was so impressed, that I have passed your organisation's name to just about everyone I chance 'pon.

Congratulations.

I was pleased that you expressed an interest in my Ketwalt Method of storytelling, and I have taken all your points on board.

What I have come up with is surely an idea which will REVOLUTIONARISE literature in the 21st and 27th centuries (I hope!).

My inspiration came a couple of years back, when I purchased a simple Binary Word Converter (BWC) from Dixons. The principle behind a BWC is pretty simple. Words are broken down to their constituent letters, each letter being assigned a numerical value. These numbers are then converted into a binary code.

Thus, prose can be laid out neatly and efficiently in binary. All the reader needs is a Reverse Binary Word Converter (RBWC), which is available from most good electrical outlets.

Here is a sample from 'He Loved Her', using the BWC method:

101 10001 1 1000 1010 1010 1001 11 11 100,
"11 1001 10 10", 1 11 1010 10
"111 111 10 10001 1". 11 1 10001 101011
11 1110 10 11.

Would your organisation be keen to spread the word of BWC? I am sure there is a market for well-written romantic novels in binary – after all, what could be better than a good romance written in code?

I look forward to your response.

Many thanks, as usual – or should I say, 110 101 11 100!!!!!

R. Li Coop

Robin Cooper

PS – I am handing in my letter of resignation next week.

END OF CORRESPONDENCE

91

Robin Cooper
Brondesbury Villas
London

Roger Dowding
The Mining Association of the United Kingdom
6 St James's Square
London SW1Y 4LD

6th April 2000

Dear Mr Dowding,

The other day whilst I was in the garden trying to fix my shed (stubborn door that won't open or close), I stumbled upon an amazing discovery that will no doubt be of interest to your organisation.

My garden is the site of an oil field. (I think).

Here's what happened: I was beating the shed door with a large shovel, when the blade came away and flew off, narrowly missing my left ear. I found the blade halfway down the garden, sticking out of the ground.

When I pulled it out, there was a huge rumbling sound. Suddenly there was a 'gush' of black sticky liquid that came out of the earth at thousands of miles an hour. It was like some HUGE FOUNTAIN, and I, Mr Dowding, got covered in the stuff. When I tasted it, I realized one thing: I had struck oil. Oil. Oil. OIL!!!! (I think).

Now my garden has been turned into an oil field (I think). My wife says it's an eye sore and keeps begging me to clean the mess up. What should I do? Perhaps I should bottle it up and try selling it on to petrol stations at a reduced rate, or maybe I should just 'burn off' the oil like they did in Iraq?

Please write back with your advice.

All the best.

Yours sincerely,

NO RESPONSE

Robin Cooper

PS – Ironically, I used some of the oil to lubricate the shed door. But it still didn't work.

Robin Cooper
Brondesbury Villas
London

Mrs C Shuttleworth
Secretary
The Society of Indexers
Mermaid House
1 Mermaid Court
London SE1 1HR

25th August 2000

Dear Mrs Shuttleworth,

I too am a fanatical indexer and always insist on arranging my shopping in alphabetical order when paying at the check-out. My clothes are hung according to the alphabet, with coats to the left, mittens in the middle and waistcoats to the right. Kitchen implements are stored according to their weight – wooded spoons on the bottom drawer, copper pots in the top. My calculators are stacked neatly with earlier models by the window, and later ones by the big basket (which is by the small basket). The medicine cupboard is arranged so that medicines manufactured in the UK are on the left, European medicines are in the middle and American medicines are on the right. My children are made to walk around the house, with my youngest, Lisa (now 10), two steps in front of me, and Michael (14) two steps behind me. Maps are filed according to their daily usefulness – with local maps at head height, foreign ones at waist level. Feelings are released within the household according to strict alphabetical rules – so feelings of anger are always released just before feelings of anxiety, which in turn are released prior to feelings of regret and remorse.

Would you like to write a piece about me in your newsletter? I am available for interviews and have been on television before.

Please don't let me down.

Keep up all the fabulous work.

Best wishes,

Robin Cooper

SOCIETY OF INDEXERS

Globe Centre, Penistone Road, Sheffield S6 3AE

Robin Cooper
Brondesbury Villas
London

10 November 2000

Dear Mr Cooper

Thank you for your letters dated 25 August and 29 September. These took some time to reach me as they were sent to the Society's old office in London.

I'm sorry, but we would not be interested in writing a piece about you in our newsletter. I think you have targeted the wrong organization. There is a bit more to indexing than arranging items into order, and I don't expect that our members would be interested in reading about your activities in this regard.

Yours sincerely

Liza Furnival
Secretary

Robin Cooper
Brondesbury Villas
London

Miss Diana B Joll
Honorary Secretary
The Silhouette Collectors Club
Brunswick Square
Hove
E Sussex

25th August 2000

Dear Diana Joll,

Am I glad to hear about you(r organisation)!

My Great Uncle, Ted Hammerns-Laapst, was one of the most influential silhouette artists in Belgium. No doubt you are aware of his work.

He not only made silhouette portraits of such eminaries as Lars Haans and Keetje Onslum, but once depicted the King and Queen (I forget their names) in their very own pantry!

I recently had a rummage around in my loft and stumbled across a number of delightful sketches made by my Great Uncle. Would you be interested in receiving a few copies?

I await your reply with great anticipation.

Best wishes,

R. Li Coq

Robin Cooper

Silhouette Collectors Club,

Brunswick Square
Hove

9th September 2000

Dear Robin Cooper,

Thank you for your very interesting letter of 25th August. Apologies for my delayed reply but I have been spending a holiday in Gloucester.

I am afraid that my knowledge of silhouette artists does not extend to those from Belgium. The Silhouette Collectors Club mostly concerns itself with artists' who worked at some point in the British Isles. This does not mean that members are not interested in silhouette artists from other countries — many are & have examples in their collections.

It is very kind of you to offer to send me copies of some of your Great Uncles' work — I would be very interested to see here. I produce a small Newsletter three times a year & it would be nice to be able to include some examples of your Great Uncle' work in the next Newsletter — due to be produced sometime in November.

Thank you for writing to me & I look forward to hearing from you faster. Do let me know if you incur any expenses in connection with the copies, postage etc as I would be pleased to refund these.

Yours sincerely,

Diane Toll
(Hon Secretary)

Robin Cooper,
Brandesbury Villas,
Wanda.

Robin Cooper
Brondesbury Villas
London

Miss Diana B Joll
Honorary Secretary
The Silhouette Collectors Club
Brunswick Square
Hove
E Sussex

13th September 2000

Dear Diana Joll,

Many great thanks for your letter of 9th September in reply to mine (of 25th August).

I was absolutely thrilled to learn that you, at the behest of your organisation, were interested in receiving copies of some of my Great Uncle (Ted Hammerns-Laapst)'s silhouette depictions.

I therefore proudly present you with a number (4) of his pictures. Please excuse the quality of the images, time is a cruel mistress to one and all.

The included pictures are as followed:

1) Dildma Juig-Thoomse, Lemberg, 1915
2) Lars Haans, Ghent, 1917
3) Prani and Limten Hammerns-Laapst, Ghent, 1921

I look forward to hearing your thoughts on my ancestor's oeuvre.

Best wishes,

Robin Cooper

Robin Cooper

PS – Regarding any expenses incurred: I did require some extra toning powder for the photocopier, but it would be insolent of me to expect recompense.

Dildma Juig-Thoomse
Lemberg 1915

Lars Haans
Ghent 1917

Prani, Zimten Hammerns-Zaapst

Ghent 1921

Robin Cooper
Brondesbury Villas
London

Ian Maclean
The Statistics Users' Council
More lane
Esher
Surrey KT10 8AP

25th August 2000

Dear Ian Maclean,

I wonder if you (or indeed one of your fine colleagues) can help.

I am currently completing a thesis on World Events, and require statistical information on a number of questions. I have heard of your fine reputation cross this bonny land and would be most grateful if you can assist.

You're my only hope.

QUESTIONS:

1) How many people in the world injure themselves each year by falling down a well?
2) How many times would you need to switch a standard light switch on and off, repeatedly until it breaks? (to nearest hundred)
3) How many lizards are there in the world?
4) How many different breeds of lizards are there:
   a) in Africa?
   b) in S.E Asia?
5) What percentage of Japanese women regularly use a hand-held fan?

I thank you in advance for all your help.

I look forward to hearing from you.

Best wishes,

Robi Coop

Robin Cooper

Sorry can't help. Sounds fascinating. I'll look forward to reading it when finishing

Best wishes

END OF CORRESPONDENCE

Robin Cooper
Brondesbury Villas
London

Mr J Arthur Parrington
General Secretary
The National Federation of Fish Friers Limited
New Federation House
4 Greenwood Mount
Meanwood
Leeds LS6 4LQ

13th May 2002

Dear Parrington (Mr),

I have heard wonderful things about your organisation, and I would therefore like to congratulate you on all that has been said to me of you.

Please excuse my impudence, I am Robin Cooper and I have been frying fish for the community at large for over 8 years (just under actually).

The reason I am writing to you is that I have devised an entirely new method of frying fish that saves on both oil and heating, resulting in an altogether less fatty product. (How often do we find ourselves enduring a greasy slab of plaice whilst suffering a *noblesse oblige* that would make even Lord Kitchener leave the room?!)

Would you care to hear of it? I hope you would.

With very best wishes, and keep up the good work.

R. Li C...

Robin Cooper

National Federation of Fish Friers Limited

New Federation House
4 Greenwood Mount
Meanwood

Leeds

LS6 4LQ

Mr R Cooper
Brondesbury Villas
LONDON

Our Ref: AMK/EMG

20 May 2002

Dear Mr Cooper

Thank you for your letter dated 13 May 2002.

I am pleased that you have heard wonderful things about the Federation, however, your sources are a little out of date. Mr Parrington retired as General Secretary in June 1998 and I am very honoured to have taken his place may I say the Federation's "first lady" at the helm!

In answer to your question "Would we care to here of your new method of frying fish?", yes. We are always ready to consider new ideas.

May I ask if you are a member of the Federation or are you in another trade?

I look forward to hearing from you as soon as possible.

Yours sincerely

Ann M Kirk (Mrs)
General Secretary

General Secretary: Mrs A Kirk - Registered in England Reg No.316379

102

Robin Cooper
Brondesbury Villas
London

Ann M Kirk (Mrs)
National Federation of Fish Friers Limited
New Federation House
4 Greenwood Mount
Meanwood
Leeds LS6 4LQ

22nd May 2002

Your (our) Ref: AMK/EMG
My (his) Ref: KAY(L*

Dear Kirk (Mrs),

Thank you so much for your wonderful letter of 20th May 2002. I cannot tell you how much joy it brought unto me. In fact I can, and I will! It really, really made my day. In fact, it also brought joy to and made the day of my wife, as she was wondering - are you the same Ann Kirk that went to her school? She would love to know.

I am sorry to hear of Parrington's retirement. I trust that this matter passed without incident. Glad to here that the NFFFL has someone so thoughtful at their helm. Welcome ab(r)oard!

Anyway, in answer to your answer to my question ("Would we (you) care to here of your (my) new method of frying fish?") I say to you this – yes!

What I do is this: I pour boiling water over ordinary wax candles. The resultant liquid is an oily substance, but perfectly safe to consume. I then dissolve flour in the mixture, until it forms a paste, and finish off the batter with a secret ingredient (sorry Ann, I can't divulge this info in this letter but I might do in my next).

Then I pop the fish (haddock or plaice for example) into this new batter and fry. It really comes up a treat. In fact, it's so popular that I have been using it to help ease tensions within my community.

I am now thinking of marketing my batter and wonder if it is OK for me to call it 'Cooper's Batter as recommended by The National Federation of Fish Friers Limited'. Would you like to attend the unveiling ceremony at Woburn Abbey in September?

I look forward to hearing from you soon – and so does my wife!

Kindest of all regards.

R. Li Coy

Robin Cooper

National Federation of Fish Friers Limited

New Federation House
4 Greenwood Mount
Meanwood

Leeds

LS6 4LQ

Mr R Cooper
Brondesbury Villas
LONDON

Our Ref: AMK/EMG

29 May 2002

Dear Mr Cooper

Thank you for your letter dated 22 May 2002.

The National President of the Federation, Adrian Herdman and I found your method for frying fish really rather interesting. I am not sure that we would be able to attend the unveiling ceremony, however, please let us have details. Again, I ask, are you the owner of a fish restaurant serving your local community?

Unfortunately, the Federation cannot "recommend or endorse" any one particular product but if you wish to name your batter "Cooper's Batter" that is up to you.

I believe I am not the same Ann Kirk who went to school with your wife as I was not a "Kirk" whilst living as a young girl in London with my parents.

Keep up the good work, happy frying!

Yours sincerely

Ann M Kirk (Mrs)
General Secretary

Ann M Kirk (Mrs)
National Federation of Fish Friers Limited
New Federation House
4 Greenwood Mount
Meanwood
Leeds LS6 4LQ

11th June 2002

Your (our) Ref: AMK/EMG
My (his) Ref: KAY(L**

Dear Kirk (Mrs),

Thank you ever so much for your speedy reply to my last letter. Such wonderful service!

I was delighted to hear that Herdman (Mr) and yourself were both interested in my new method of frying fish. Most people are soon won round – you too it seems.

You asked whether "you (I) are (am) the owner of a fish restaurant serving your (my) local community?". That's a good question – I do indeed operate from a 'base' from which I fry fish for the local community, although the 'base' is quite unspecific as such. My local community don't seem to mind – on the contrary – they have more than got used to it over the years. I hope this clarifies the situation.

My wife was disappointed to read that you were not the same Ann Kirk who attended her school. What a shame! The Ann Kirk she remembers actually moved to Canada where she married an optician. I believe she later returned to England, only to marry again.

I am pleased that you liked the name 'Cooper's Batter', and all seems to be going well for the Unveiling Ceremony. It's a pity such honoured guests as yourselves won't be able to make it. I already have both the French and Norwegian ambassadors attending, along with the great, great granddaughter of Gustav Klimt. It should be a wonderful evening. Perhaps you would reconsider.

Would you like me to print your organisation's name on the literature?

I look forward to hearing from you and thank you for your kindness.

Best wishes,

Robin Cooper

PS – I promised to let you know the name of the 'secret' ingredient. Would you still like to know it?

National Federation of Fish Friers Limited

New Federation House
4 Greenwood Mount
Meanwood

Leeds
LS6 4LQ

Mr R Cooper
Brondesbury Villas
LONDON

Our Ref: AMK/EMG

18 June 2002

Dear Mr Cooper

Thank you for your letter dated 11 June 2002.

You say in your letter that you operate from a "base" where you fry fish for the local community, I do not feel that your answer has clarified my question. I would be grateful if you could be more specific and answer my original question.

Unfortunately, it is not Federation policy to either allow companies to use the logo on their products or recommend specific manufacturers of branded goods.

Your "secret ingredient" must be good, do you wish us to know it?

May I wish you every success in keeping your community happy. Happy frying!

Yours sincerely

Ann M Kirk (Mrs)
General Secretary

Ann M Kirk (Mrs)
National Federation of Fish Friers Limited
New Federation House
4 Greenwood Mount
Meanwood
Leeds LS6 4LQ

21st June 2002

Your (our) Ref: AMK/EMG
My (his) Ref: KAY(L***

Dear Kirk (Mrs),

I thank you once again for such a fantastic service. I'm not talking about Wimbledon(!),
I mean your ability to reply so promptly – and with such kind words.

I apologise for being unspecific regarding my 'base'. The reason I use this word is
because people in my community refer to it as 'The Base'. It has 'The Base' written
in coloured letters on it, hence the name. I trust this makes things clearer.

Following your last letter, you will be pleased to know that I have removed your
organisation's name from my literature (I just made it to the printers in time!). I have
also scrapped my plans of printing a giant picture of yourself on the front of the base,
since I feel from the tone of your letter, that this might displease you. "But how do
you know what I look like?!" I hear you ask. Well, I don't. So I was going to hazard a
guess. My intention was to paint a rather elegant lady wearing a red jumper, 'sleek'
shoes, and sporting a monocle. Was I close?

You will be pleased to know that I can reveal my 'secret' ingredient. It's basically
nothing more than common Thamibin. Do you think we could link up and start
marketing this new method?

I look forward to hearing from you – and to you I say – HAPPY FRYING!!!

All the very best,

Robin Cooper

END OF CORRESPONDENCE

Robin Cooper
Brondesbury Villas
London

Lauren Milsom
Secretary
The National Left-Handers Association
Brewer Street
London

11th June 2002

Dear Lauren,

Please do not be alarmed. The shoddiness of my writing is not due to illness rather an experiment I am carrying out to bring awareness to the plight of left-handed people.

I myself am a right-handed individual, but my wife is the opposite – left-handed. She has suffered both name-calling and hair-pulling on account of the way she holds a pen.

To demonstrate against this injustice, I am planning to write only with my left hand for the next 12 months. Would you support my campaign? Perhaps you would print my letter in your newsletter.

I look forward to hearing from you.
Best wishes,
Robin Cooper

Robin Cooper
Brondesbury Villas
London

Mrs Lorna Smith
Secretary
The Stair Society
Saltire Court
20 Castle Terrace
Edinburgh
EH1 2ET

11th June 2002

Dear Mrs Smith,

Since 1992, I have been keeping a record of the number of stairs I climb each day. I have all the figures neatly tabulated in a specially adapted diary, with each entry clearly indexed, for ease of cross-referencing.

I am currently looking to get my 'Stair Diaries' published, as I feel they would make an interesting read. I wonder if this is something The Stair Society would like to get behind. Would you like to read a proof of my book? Perhaps you would consider writing the foreword.

I look forward to hearing from you, and keep up all the good work.

With very best wishes,

Robin Cooper

THE STAIR SOCIETY

Instituted in 1934 to encourage the study and to advance the knowledge of the history of Scots Law

President: The Right Hon the Lord Hope of Craighead PC LLD

Secretary & Treasurer
THOMAS H DRYSDALE WS

SALTIRE COURT
20 CASTLE TERRACE
EDINBURGH
EH1 2ET

12 June 2002

Our Ref: S0422001/JC/MHR

Robin Cooper, Esq
Brondesbury Villas
London

Dear Mr Cooper

The Stair Society

Thank you for your letter of 11 June 2002.   Unfortunately, I do not think that the Society is relevant to your cause as The Stair Society was established in 1934 to encourage the study and advance the knowledge of Scots law.

I wish you every success with the publishing of your diary.

Yours sincerely

Janine Christie.

Janine Christie
Trust Administrator

END OF CORRESPONDENCE

Robin Cooper
Brondesbury Villas
London

Gillian Allder
National Cavity Insulation Association
PO Box 12
Haslemere
Surrey
GU27 3AH

10th January 2003

Dear Gillian,

Happy New Year!!!!!

Please allow me to introduce myself. I am Robin Cooper, loft insulator and poet.

I have been insulating lofts for over 9 years (nearer 11 really) and in my spare time I also write poems. This one is called 'Nice and Warm'. Would you like to publish it in your newsletter?*

NICE AND WARM by Robin Cooper

Up the stairs,
In the loft,
Cold air, cold air,
Cold air wafts.

So I come,
To your help,
Insulating,
The loft itself,

Now it is,
Nice and warm,
I'll have a cuppa',
I'm up at dawn!

Hope you like it and I look forward to hearing from you.

Best wishes,

Robin Cooper
* If you don't have a newsletter, I'm happy to become your 'Poet in Residence'!

NATIONAL CAVITY INSULATION ASSOCIATION

PO Box 12, Haslemere, Surrey GU27 3AH

Director (Exec): Gillian A. Allder MIPR, MIAM

GA/ldo

14 January, 2003

Mr Robin Cooper
Brodesbury Villas
London

Dear Mr Cooper,

Thank you for introducing yourself. Would you be interested in becoming a member? Best wishes with your poetry. We are not in a position to publish currently.

Yours sincerely

Gillian A. Allder

Gillian A Allder
NATIONAL INSULATION ASSOCIATION LTD

Robin Cooper
Brondesbury Villas
London

Gillian Allder
National Cavity Insulation Association
PO Box 12
Haslemere
Surrey
GU27 3AH

24th January 2003

Your ref: GA/Ido
My ref: Letter to National Cavity Insulation Association (2)

Dear Gillian Allder,

Hearty thanks for your charming letter of 14th January regarding my poetry. Thank you also for wishing me "best wishes" for my poetry. I shall take them (your best wishes) to heart!!!!

Many thanks in addition for inviting me to become a member of your wonderful organisation. I am flattered to be asked and, of course, duly accept.

Could you please forward me details of the joining ceremony, i.e. when this will be taking place, at what time, and what I should wear for the occasion (I was hoping to wear my red tunic – is this alright?). Finally, I would like to know whether this invitation extends to my wife, as she would love to see me being enrolled.

Looking forward to hearing from you,

Best wishes,

Robin Cooper

NATIONAL **CAVITY INSULATION** ASSOCIATION

PO Box 12, Haslemere, Surrey GU27 3AH

Director (Exec): Gillian A. Allder MIPR, MIAM

28 January, 2003

TO: Robin Cooper
From: Gillian Allder, NIA

Re Membership:

Thanks for letter of January 24th. We are a trade association funded by our members. Regrettably we did not offer membership, but an application pack. The subscription is £333 + VAT for the remainder of the year until September 30. Is this of interest please?

Regards

Robin Cooper
Brondesbury Villas
London

Gillian Allder
National Cavity Insulation Association
PO Box 12
Haslemere
Surrey
GU27 3AH

6th February 2003

Dear Gillian,

Many thanks for your swift reply (28th January) to my letter of 4 days previous. I should like to say that I am most impressed at your organisation.

Unfortunately, I must admit that I was extremely upset* to learn that I have had my membership revoked. Why is this so? What have I done? My wife is now totally distraught and feels, as she puts it, "a laughing stock amongst the insulation community".

I beg you to reconsider.

Perhaps my wife and I should visit your headquarters to talk over this matter. Luckily we will be in Haslemere on Monday 3rd March, as my wife has an appointment with a milliner (hat-maker). Are you free at around 3:30pm?

I look forward to hearing from you.

Best wishes,

Robin Cooper

* As a poet, I am a sensitive type.

NATIONAL **CAVITY INSULATION** ASSOCIATION

PO Box 12, Haslemere, Surrey GU27 3AH

Director (Exec): Gillian A. Allder MIPR, MIAM

GA/ldo   11 February, 2003

Mr Robin Cooper
Brondesbury Villas
London

Dear Mr Cooper,

Membership:

Please understand we have not revoked a membership that was not offered in the first place. Membership application (which has not been made) is always subject to acceptance by our Council and payment of subscription. Regret I am not available for further discussion on this.

Best wishes.

Yours sincerely

a. andy

Gillian A Allder
NATIONAL INSULATION ASSOCIATION LTD

National Cavity Insulation Association Limited - by guarantee: trading as NCIA

116

Robin Cooper
Brondesbury Villas
London

Gillian Allder
National Cavity Insulation Association
PO Box 12
Haslemere
Surrey
GU27 3AH

14th February 2003

Dear Gillian,

Many thanks for your letter of 11th February. Again the efficiency of your organisation has been noted.

In the meantime, my wife and I look forward to seeing you on Monday 3rd March at 3:30 pm. I would be grateful if you could advise me as to the parking conditions around your offices, or better still, reserve me a parking space in your forecourt, should you have one.

Many thanks,

Until then,

Best wishes,

Robin Cooper

NCIA

NATIONAL **CAVITY INSULATION** ASSOCIATION

PO Box 12, Haslemere, Surrey GU27 3AH

Director (Exec): Gillian A. Allder MIPR, MIAM

GA/ldo

18 February, 2003

Robin Cooper
Brondesbury Villas
London

Dear Robin,

Thank you for your letter. Regret we are not in a position to meet you due to commitments to our members.

Yours sincerely

Gillian A Allder
NATIONAL INSULATION ASSOCIATION LTD

END OF CORRESPONDENCE

National Cavity Insulation Association Limited - by guarantee: trading as NCIA

Robin Cooper
Brondesbury Villas
London

Ros Beattie
Keep Fit Association
Suite 105
Astra House
Arklow Road
London SE14 6EB

10th February 2003

Dear Ros,

Are you fit? Can you do 200 press-ups without losing your breath? Can you? Can you? Can you Ros?

Please excuse my impertinence, but I can. That's because I've been developing a new form of 'Keep Fit' which I believe will REVOLUTIONARIZE the entire 'Keep Fit' industry.

Wanna hear about it? I bet that you do want to.

It's called LIONEL ISSON'S EXPATION TECHNIQUE (OF KEEP FIT), or LIET(OKF). It's based on Lionel Isson's programme of cardio-vascular exercises which were very popular in Japan in the early 80's.

LIET(OKF) requires the individual to work in pairs, both of whom use designated weights, or 'Jansens' to improve circulation ('Thaa-Henty'). Each Jansen is measured in 'Paarns', with each Paarn indirectly proportional to the rate, or 'Yintopson', of Thaa-Henty. The total Yintopson, is calculated via simple maths to work out the exact Thaa-Henty achieved.

Would you like me to send you a chart depicting the various exercises used in LIET(OKF)? I'd love to have your organisation's backing.

I guarantee that this is a REVOLUTION in 'Keep Fit' and look forward to hearing from you.

Yours sincerely,

Robin Cooper

NO RESPONSE

Robin Cooper
Brondesbury Villas
London

Mr D P Dossett
Electrical Installation Equipment Manufacturers' Association Ltd
Westminster Tower
3 Albert Embankment
London SE1 7SL

25th February 2003

Dear Mr Dossett,

What a long name your organisation has - it occupies over half the page – horizontally!

That is beside the point, and I trust that you do not mind my little joke.

I have heard that your organisation is extremely well-organised, well-run and very, very helpful. In fact I have countless affidavits as to this effect (which I am more than happy to show you). Hence my writing to you.

I wonder if you would be able to furnish me with some assistance:

I am seeking a number of components for my wife's 'hair station'. You may be aware of 'hair-stations' – I believe most women of a certain age possess one – they're rather large, cumbersome and often noisy – and I'm not talking about the women!!! Anyway, I have been unable to locate any of these components and my wife is in a terrible state.

Here they (the components) are: (Please excuse my artwork):

1) Valve? 9 mm across. Serial no 1/980 – D (I think it is Dutch)
2) Bolt. 25 cm x 0.9 cm. Company name 'Kjelpart'.
3) Copper wiring. Size fluctuates between 1 cm – 90 cm. Has the words 'Lisp Henry' scratched on the underside.

I would be grateful if you could provide me with any help as to where I can find these items.

Many thanks in advance.

Best wishes,

Robin Cooper

Robin Cooper

Rapier House,
40-46 Lamb's Conduit Street
London WC1N 3NW

11 March 2003

Mr Robin Cooper
Brondesbury Villas
London

Dear Mr Cooper,

I write with reference to the letter you sent to Mr D P Dossett at EIEMA (enclosed), with regard to your request for information on spare parts for your wife's "hair station". I regret that Mr Dossett's association does not cover such products (despite its long name) and he has passed your letter to us – The Association of Manufacturers of Domestic Appliances – AMDEA for short!

Whilst such products as hair stations or hair dryers fall within our remit I regret to advise you that from the information you have provided it has proved impossible to identify the maker or supplier of the parts you describe so carefully. There is however one further port of call which you could try, that is the Small Electrical Appliances Marketing Association - SEAMA for short! Their address is: Ambassador House, Brigstock Road, Thornton Heath, Surrey, CR7 7JG.

I am sorry we have been unable to help you further.

Yours sincerely

Ian M. Lucking
Association Executive.

Robin Cooper
Brondesbury Villas
London

SEAMA (The Small Electrical Appliances Marketing Association) *
Ambassador House
Brigstock Road
Thornton Heath
Surrey
CR7 7JG

13th March 2003

Dear Sir/Madam,

As you can see from the enclosed correspondence, I wrote to EIEMA on 25th February. EIEMA passed my letter on to AMDEA (some time between 26th February and 11th March), and AMDEA wrote back to me on 11th March, recommending I write to you – SEAMA, which I am therefore doing (on 13th March).

I wonder if you could be of help.

As you can see from my enclosed letters, I am desperately seeking a variety of components for my wife's 'hair station'. I trust the diagrams on my letter to EIEMA are self-explanatory.

Can you help?

I look forward to hearing from you and thank you, in advance, for your assistance.

Best wishes,

[signature]

Robin Cooper

* You too have a very long name – it also occupies over half the page – horizontally!

Small Electrical Appliance Marketing Association

Orbital House, 85 Croydon Road, Caterham, Surrey CR3 6PD.

08 May 2003
SE

Mr Robin Cooper
Brondesbury Villas
London

Dear Mr Cooper

Thank you for your letter dated 13 March 2003 requesting information on spare parts. I would like to apologise for the delay in responding to you.

I am afraid that we also have been unable to identify the manufacturer of your wife's hair station and therefore we are unable to help you.

I am sorry that we have not been able to help you on this occasion, but wish you luck in your search.

Yours sincerely

CHARLOTTE HARMER
<u>SEAMA</u>

A private company Limited by Guarantee.   Registered Office: Orbital House, 85 Croydon Road, Caterham, Surrey CR3 6PD
Registered in England.   Company Number 1667836.   VAT Registration Number 306 7195 58

Robin Cooper
Brondesbury Villas
London

Jenny Rosser
President
The National Association of Pension Funds Ltd
NIOC House
4 Victoria Street
London SW1H 0NX

26th April 2003

Dearest Jenny,

I have heard so many smashing things said of your organisation. Comments range from "very kind", "thoughtful" and "benevolent to a 't'!".

Bearing all that in mind, I have a pension-related query that I am sure you will be able to answer, and trust that, in doing so, you do not waste too much time on me!

With the onset of pension relief funding tied to a dividend forecast in relation to the buying or selling of loan assisted gilts, coupled with a capped equity market whose variable rate of interest is set against a 'pivoting' investment fund, indirectly linked to the standard base rate of a tax-free pension subsidiary, would I need to advise the Inland Revenue of the exact whereabouts of the so-called 'Tim-Haal-Kaypom'?

I look forward to your response, and thank you once again.

With very best wishes,

In yours, I remain,

Robin Cooper

Cc Lord Rothermere

The Pensions
Management
Institute

Pensions Professionals
in practice

SMH/SMW

R Cooper Esq
Brondesbury Villas
LONDON

9 July 2003

Dear Mr Cooper

Thank you for your letter of 6 July.

I am sorry we cannot help with your query.

Yours sincerely

Susan M Howlett
Secretary General

END OF CORRESPONDENCE

Jim Winship
Director
The Event Services Association
Home Farm
Ardington
Oxon

25th May 2003

Dear Mr Winship,

I am a Children's Entertainer and have heard many wonderful things said about your said organisation. From what I understand, you represent the interests of those employed in the party and events world.

That is why I am writing to you...

My name is Robin Cooper but my Children's Entertainer's name is ICARUS. Why 'Icarus'? I hear you ask. Well, my act is based on the life of Icarus, that's why. If you recall, Icarus was the Roman man who tried to fly by donning a coat of many feathers and flapping about too near to the sun.

Here's what I do: I turn up at children's parties dressed, like Icarus, in feathers. Every part of my body is encased in the stuff – even my face is completely feathered (not bad for an asthma sufferer!).

I start a small fire in a metal dustbin which I place on top of a shelf or cupboard, and explain that this represents the sun. I then ask all the children to chant:

> 'Icarus, Icarus,
> Thou artst,
> The flying man'

Once they have been worked up into a frenzy (it's so easy with kids) I take out my step ladder and proceed to flap my wings. The children are then instructed to chant:

> 'Icarus, Icarus,
> Flap thy wings,
> Master of the light'

It is at this point that I quickly go over the fire procedure, usually appointing the birthday boy or girl as Fire monitor. As I begin to mount the ladder, the children are ordered to chant:

> 'Climb thy rung,
> Thou sturdy knight,
> O Icarus, Icarus,
> Make thy flight'

I then command the children to stop breathing until I reach the top (usually only about 45-60 seconds).

continued overleaf

At the 'summit' I spread my wings and the children release their tiny, little breaths. They proclaim:

> 'O Icarus, Icarus,
> Thy wings of gold,
> The flying man,
> Thou artst so bold'

The children are made to count down from 100 in Roman numerals. As soon as they reach 1 (or 'I'), I leap off the ladder into the flaming dustbin. As I come crashing down, the Fire Monitor steps forward and puts out the flames with the extinguisher.

The children hold hands and chant:

> 'Hail Icarus,
> Fool of the light,
> Thy trip to the sun,
> Was a deadly flight'

That, in a nutshell, is my act. Icarus – Children's Entertainer.

Can I go straight ahead and use The Events Services Association's name on my promotional material as I'm having some new leaflets printed up in a couple of weeks time? I assume that I will qualify for membership.

I look forward to hearing from you.

Best wishes,

Robin Cooper

03 June 2003

Mr Robin Cooper
Brondesbury Villas
London

Dear Mr Cooper

Thank you for your letter of 25th May 2003.

Unfortunately you need to apply to be a TESA member before we can allow you to use the TESA logo
on literature etc.

Enclosed is a membership application form and details. The lowest cost way you could join would be
as an event organiser.

If you would like any further information, please do not hesitate to call us.

Yours sincerely

Jim Winship
Director

Robin Cooper
Brondesbury Villas
London

Jim Winship
Director
The Event Services Association
Lower Church Street
Chepstow
Monmouthshire

4th June 2003

Dear Mr Winship,

Many thanks for replying to my letter of 25th May on 3rd June. I was greatly touched.

If you recall, I am ICARUS ('The Flying Man').

I was saddened to learn that I would not be able to use your organisation's name on my literature

So….

I have taken the liberty of sending you a rough copy of the type of promotional material I will be sending out. You will notice that your association's name is quite small on the page, and the quote pretty generic (if you saw my show, I know you would say what I wrote!).

Now that you have all the facts in front of you, I am really hoping you will change your mind and give it your approval. It would mean so much to me – and my wife.

Fingers crossed. I go to print in three weeks!

In yours I humbly remain,

Robin Cooper

FOR THE VERY BEST IN EVENTS…

IT HAS TO BE…..

ICARUS
('The Flying Man')

Children's Parties
Weddings
Hospital 'walkabouts'
Loft Conversion ceremonies

And LOTS more…

"Never have we seen such a show. Wonderful stuff!"

The entire staff of
The Events Services Association

The Event Services Association

Picton House, Lower Church Street,
Monmouthshire

05 June 2003

Mr Robin Cooper
Brondesbury Villas
London

Dear Mr Cooper

Thank you for your letter.

Unfortunately, there is no way we can allow you to use the TESA name or logo as an endorsement for your business unless you are a member and have suitable references. Even then we would never allow you to use the wording you have set out on your leaflet as it is highly misleading – our staff have never even seen your show and have no knowledge of you.

I would also advise you to be extremely careful about the wording you use on your leaflet as inferences such as this could get you into trouble with Trading Standards.

I do not want to discourage you but you should take care.

Yours sincerely

Jim Winship
Director

END OF CORRESPONDENCE

130

Robin Cooper
Brondesbury Villas
London

John Alexander
Chairman
Association of Small Historic Towns & Villages of the United Kingdom
5 Upper St Martin's Lane
London WC2H 9EA

26th May 2003

Dear Mr Alexander,

I am a great admirer of your organisation, and think that you do good, honest work for the community (and communities) at large (and little!).

I wonder if you can help.

I have devised a new marketing idea specifically designed to promote the small towns and villages of this glorious isle. Would you be interested in having a look at it (the idea)?

I do hope so.

With very best wishes,

Forward with small towns and villages!

[signature]

Robin Cooper

5 Upper St. Martin's Lane
London
WC2H 9EA

5th June, 2003

R. Cooper, Esq.,
Brondesbury Villas,
London.

Dear Mr. Cooper,

Thank you for your letter of 26th May. I would be more than happy to discuss your marketing idea to promote small towns and villages in the U.K.

Please give me a ring to discuss this further.

Yours faithfully,

J.B. Alexander
Chairman
ASHTAV

Robin Cooper
Brondesbury Villas
London

John Alexander
Chairman
Association of Small Historic Towns & Villages of the United Kingdom
5 Upper St Martin's Lane
London WC2H 9EA

7th June 2003

Dear Mr Alexander,

Many thanks for such a swift response to my correspondence. It did not go unnoticed.

Thank you also for showing such interest in my marketing idea for small historic towns and villages of the United Kingdom. I'm afraid that I am unable to call you as I do not own a phone, and since I am not entirely sure how to operate a public phone box, I would prefer to write to you. I trust you do not mind.

My idea for the marketing of small historic towns and villages of the United Kingdom is pretty simple. I have now acquired the rights to the popular figure, 'Parmaynu'. No doubt you are aware of his attributes, so I won't bore you with them. Nevertheless, Parmaynu is a much-loved and trusted character.

Through a series of posters, promoted by Parmaynu, we can get the message across that small historic towns and villages are there for ALL of us to be enjoyed. We can also promote your organisation with details of membership fees.

I have designed a dummy poster (enclosed) which I am planning to affix to trees and vehicles in my local area over the next few weeks. Are you ready to go with the idea?

I look forward to hearing from you,

Best wishes,

Robin Cooper

Robin Cooper

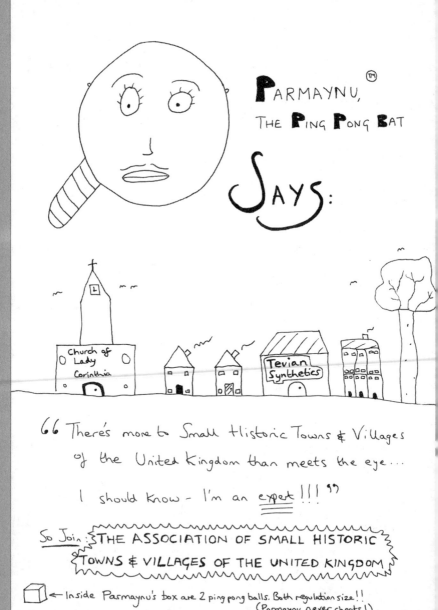

PARMAYNU,™
THE PING PONG BAT

SAYS:

66 There's more to Small Historic Towns & Villages
of the United Kingdom than meets the eye...

I should know - I'm an expert !!! 99

So Join: THE ASSOCIATION OF SMALL HISTORIC
TOWNS & VILLAGES OF THE UNITED KINGDOM

← Inside Parmaynu's box are 2 ping pong balls. Both regulation size !!
(Parmaynu never cheats !)

10th June, 2003

R. Cooper, Esq.,
Brondesbury Villas,
London.

Dear Mr. Cooper,

ASHTAV

Thank you for your letter of 7th June.

I am afraid that your idea holds no interest whatsoever for us and I would be grateful if you could cease to correspond with me.

Yours sincerely,

J.B. Alexander
Chairman
ASHTAV

END OF CORRESPONDENCE

135

Robin Cooper
Brondesbury Villas
London

Dr Ken Lee
Secretary
The Ball & Roller Bearing Manufacturers Association
Birmingham

26th May 2003

Dear Doctor Lee,

My son Michael is ball-bearing mad, and has been collecting them for years. He now owns 95,000 ball-bearings. Michael has catalogued each and every one by size, weight, date of purchase and luminescence. These figures fill the pages of 300 notebooks.

As a ball-bearing man, perhaps you can help.

I have recently told Michael that he has to curb his hobby – not only does it take over the whole house, but his ball-bearings are a complete hazard (my wife re-broke her ankle after slipping on one recently).

Michael has threatened to flood the house when we are out if we so much as touch one of his bearings.

My wife and I are at our wits end. Can you help?

Perhaps you could pen a short note to my son to ask him to cut down on his ball-bearing collection. I am sure that he would respect you, as you are at the pinnacle of the ball-bearing world (and a doctor).

Many thanks in advance.

I look forward to hearing from you,

Best wishes,

Robin Cooper

Robin Cooper

10 June 2003

Luton
ENGLAND

Mr Michael Cooper
Brondesbury Villas
London

Dear Michael

It is with great sadness that we receive the news that your parents are being unreasonably intolerant of your harmless and educational hobby of collecting ball bearings.

We wholeheartedly support you in this venture and I have enclosed several publications aimed at helping you in packing, storing, lubricating and caring for your impressive collection in the most appropriate fashion.

Of course, the extent of your collection also brings with it some responsibilities towards your parents and any visitors to the house, under the current Health and Safety legislation. To this end I have enclosed leaflets on the best practices and if you would like some assistance in acquiring the most fashionable of work wear and safety equipment, at discounted prices, please be in contact. Most importantly you should equip your long suffering mother with some decent safety shoes.

I am also concerned that you may not be acquiring your stock from authorised distributors of the major brands. It is most important that you cease this practice immediately, if this is the case, as it would rapidly devalue the investment in your collection if the quality were anything but the best throughout. You should also be on the look out for fraudulent markings and unapproved logo usage.

Could I also ask that you withdraw your threat to flood the house, if the collection were to be disturbed. This could have a disastrous effect on the life of the products as well as making your superb documentation exceedingly soggy.

If we can be of any further help please keep in touch. Naturally the bearings industry is only too aware of its environmental responsibilities so it is incumbent on you to let us know if you wish to divest yourself of the collection, or indeed if you just decide to grow up, so that appropriate steps can be taken.

Yours sincerely

C F Trotman
Director of SKF (U.K.) Limited and
Chairman
Ball and Rolling Bearing Manufacturers Association

END OF CORRESPONDENCE

SKF (U.K.) Limited
Sundon Park Road, Luton,
Bedfordshire LU3 3BL.

Registered Office
Sundon Park Road, Luton,
Bedfordshire LU3 3BL.

Registered in
England
No. 107367

Lode Williams
Belgian Ambassador to the UK
The Belgian Embassy
103 Eaton Square
London SW1W 9AB

2nd January 2004

Dear Ambassador,

This is the first time I have ever written to an Ambassador, so please do excuse my nerves.

I recently set out on a single holiday to your beautiful country of Belgium. I normally travel with my wife and children but felt I needed to be alone for a couple of months. I won't bore you with all the reasons – some are financial, others more personal. Nevertheless, I suffered extreme discrimination on account of me being a single traveller.

I checked into a quaint hotel – La Taverne de Mystecles, just outside of Bruges. When I informed the receptionist that I wanted a single room, I was met with such a haughty look, that I felt as if I would turn into Mystecles herself! Not wanting to cause a scene, I agreed to their terms, and found myself signing a lengthy document in which I agreed to share a room with a total stranger.

That stranger was none other than Monsieur Ybert Tali…

Naturally I was aware of his reputation (who isn't!), but was unaware that Monsieur Tali was also a chronic sleep-walker. Thus, in the middle of the night, I awoke to find Monsieur Tali clambering out of the 4th floor bedroom window, wearing my suit. I saved him but not, alas, his reputation. It goes without saying that I was summarily thrown out of the hotel. My belongings destroyed in a furnace.

When I complained, I was met with a barrage of abuse, including one phrase which roughly translates as "poor water boy".

Can you help? I feel that my case should be heard.

I look forward to hearing from you.

With very best wishes for the year (2004) ahead.

Robin Cooper

NO RESPONSE

Dr Simon Thurley
Chief Executive
English Heritage
23 Savile Row
London W1S 2ET

7th January 2004

Dear Doctor,

I wonder if you can help?

From what I understand – and I quote – 'English Heritage is a statutory body which gives grants to thousands of listed buildings, cathedrals, churches, archaeological sites, historic parks and gardens and ancient monuments across England, incorporating the National Monuments Record'.

Well that is some achievement, and you certainly get my vote!

I'll get to my point. I am looking for a small grant (around £12,000 – £90,000) for my latest project, which I feel is of enormous BENEFIT to this nation of ours.

I am planning to erect a giant tent (see diagram), constructed out of fabric and concrete that will stand for 50 years as a testament to the popular figure, 'Parmaynu'. I need not go into the wheres and hows of Parmaynu's worth to this fayre land – needless to say that I foresee this will become a LANDMARK and a TOURIST ATTRACTION for 60 years at least!

The location of the tent ('Parmaynuville') will ideally be situated right opposite Buckingham Palace (possibly to replace the old statue that everyone climbs on), but these are mere details at this stage.

I trust you will study my plans, and hopefully give me the nod.

I look forward to hearing from you.

Best wishes,

R. Li Coy

Robin Cooper

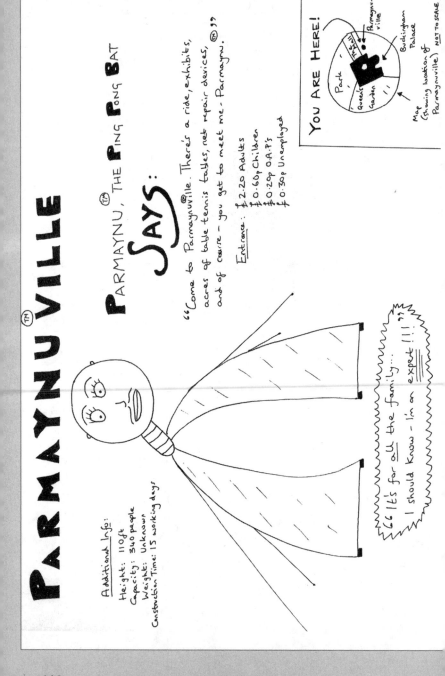

from the Chief Executive
Dr Simon Thurley

Our ref: TO 742

Mr Robin Cooper
Brondesbury Villas
London

12 January 2004

Dear Mr Cooper

Thank you for your letter of 7 January addressed to Dr Simon Thurley, Chief Executive of English Heritage, regarding your project to raise £12,000 – £90,000 in order to erect a giant tent opposite Buckingham Palace.

Dr Thurley has asked me to forward your letter to Philip Davies, Regional Director, London Region, who will arrange for a reply to be sent on his behalf.

Yours sincerely

Maxine White
Chief Executive's Office

The National Monuments Record is the public archive of English Heritage

ENGLISH HERITAGE

Mr Robin Cooper
Brondesbury Villas
London

16th January 2004

Dear Mr Cooper

'PARMAYNUVILLE' PROJECT

You will have already heard from Maxine White of Simon Thurley's office that your letter of 7th January was passed to Philip Davies, the director of London Region of English Heritage who has, in turn, asked me to provide you with a short reply on his behalf.

While you are right that English Heritage gives grants and advice for a whole range of heritage projects, I'm afraid that your scheme would not be considered to fall within any of these categories. I suggest, however, that since the mission you outline and so vividly illustrate seems to celebrate the joys of table tennis it would probably be more appropriately funded from a source such as the Sports Lottery Fund.

To get a overall idea of how your proposal would be received it might anyway be worth your contacting the Department for Culture Media and Sport (DCMS) for a steer over the inevitable planning issues it would raise. For example: any proposal for a site in the park near Buckingham Palace (and certainly one involving alteration to the Victoria Memorial) would have to have the approval of the Westminster City Council planners and the Royal Household.

On behalf of both our Chief Executive and the Director of London Region I am sorry to have to direct your appeal for assistance away from English Heritage, especially in the light of your evident enthusiasm for our role in supporting and promoting the heritage of this country.

Yours sincerely,

John Thorneycroft LVO

Head of Government Historic Estates Unit

c. Simon Thurley, Philip Davies.

END OF CORRESPONDENCE

23 SAVILE ROW LONDON W1S 2ET

The National Monuments Record is the public archive of English Heritage

Robin Cooper
Brondesbury Villas
London

Mrs Wendy Barry
The British Hamster Association
PO Box 825
Sheffield
S Yorks
S17 3RU

7th January 2004

Dear Barry,

Hope is at hand! (At least I HOPE so!!).

I wonder if you can help…

I have a beautiful hamster named 'Hambles' who is coming up to his 4th birthday.

Hambles has to be the most talented of all hamsters, in that he can communicate with me via his scratching. By repeatedly clawing at a piece of fabric, Hambles can communicate up to 80 words and phrases. In fact, Hambles has already been featured on Swiss Television, where he garnered much fan mail.

Would you be interested to hear more of Hambles?

I look forward to hearing from you.

Best wishes,

Robin Cooper

Robin Cooper

BRITISH HAMSTER ASSOCIATION
Secretary: Wendy Barry. Stonebridge Drive, Frome, Somerset.

PO Box 825, Sheffield,
S17 3RU, England

Hello Robin,

Many thanks for your letter to the BHA regarding your hamster 'Hambles'.

I have to be honest I was a little sceptical on hearing about a hamster being able to communicate in such a way, however I would be very interested to hear more, why not drop me a line or email.

You say in your letter that your hamster is coming up for his 4th birthday, this is remarkable in itself as the average life span for a Syrian hamster is 2 years, very occasional they get to 3 years, but most are dead by 3 years.

I enclose some information leaflets which I hope will be useful to you.

Best wishes

Wendy

Wendy Barry (Mrs)

Robin Cooper
Brondesbury Villas
London

Mrs Wendy Barry
The British Hamster Association
PO Box 825
Sheffield
S Yorks S17 3RU

28th January 2004

Dear Barry,

Many thanks for your delightful letter in response to my previous correspondence.

I must begin with a apology (or rather 'an' apology!!!). I stated very clearly in my letter that Hambles was coming up to his 4th birthday. However, this was an error committed by me, as Hambles, is alas, nearly 2. In other words, Hambles is approaching his 2nd birthday. (We hold it on 6th February).

Please accept my apology. I should have re-read my letter before it was sent. I did not, and can only LEARN from my experience.

And so we move on.

You asked to hear more of Hambles' talents. Here are but a few:

If I ask Hambles to count the number of people there are in my room, (say there are 15) he will scratch the amount onto a piece of fabric, which we call 'Yes Felt' (i.e. he scratches the Yes Felt 15 times, and NOT the figure '15' – not even Hambles can do that!).

A man with glasses walks past our window every morning, who we believe to be Mr Turner. Hambles scratches 8 times, signifying the figure '8' - the shape of Mr Turner's glasses.

Whenever Hambles wants to go to sleep at night, he scratches twice on the Yes Felt (i.e 'Good Night').

Many thanks and also many thanks for the leaflets you enclosed.

Best wishes,

Robin Cooper
Robin Cooper

END OF CORRESPONDENCE

Robin Cooper
Brondesbury Villas
London

Councillor Robert Davis
Executive Chairman
The London Mayors' Association
c/o Freeman Box & Co
8 Bentinck Street
London W1U 2BJ

7th January 2004

Dear Councillor Robert Davis,

Happy New(ish) year,

I have always taken a keen interest in civic affairs (in fact for 4 years I ran a catering company that supplied sundry items to the local mayor on a day-to-day basis – mainly general foodstuffs – cereals, milk, bread etc.) and have become fascinated with the glorious tradition of perhaps the mayor's most important civic item: the mace.

I have made some significant changes to the design of the mace, which I feel could be adopted nationally. I would love to show you my designs, and wonder if this is possible.

I look forward to hearing from you.

Best wishes,

Robin Cooper

Robin Cooper

THE LONDON MAYORS ASSOCIATION

[Established in 1901]

Chairman: The Lord Mayor of Westminster

President: Hon Alderman Mrs Margaret Calcott-James   Executive Chairman: Councillor Robert Davis

8 Bentinck Street, London W1U 2BJ

Robin Cooper Esq
Brondesbury Villas
London

14th January 2004

Dear Mr Cooper

Thank you for your letter of 7th January 2004.

I enclose herewith a copy of our Newsletter in case you have not received a copy yourself.

I would be happy to discuss with you the question of a mace and suggest you contact me so that we can arrange a meeting.

Yours sincerely

COUNCILLOR ROBERT DAVIS
EXECUTIVE CHAIRMAN
THE LONDON MAYORS' ASSOCIATION

Enc.

RD/SM/LMA4/Jan/58c

The London Mayors' Association is a Company limited by guarantee
and registered under company number: 3682500

147

Robin Cooper
Brondesbury Villas
London

Councillor Robert Davis
Executive Chairman
The London Mayors' Association
c/o Freeman Box & Co
8 Bentinck Street
London W1U 2BJ

15th January 2004

Dear Councillor Robert Davis,

Many thanks for your swift reply (14th January) to my letter (7th January). I only wish more people could be as diligent as your good self. Thank you again.

I am glad you were interested to hear of my new designs for the traditional mace. You also kindly asked me to call you on the number you provided. Unfortunately I am unable to call you at the moment, as I am currently recovering from a rather nasty accident I suffered whilst visiting a local glue plant. I trust you understand.

That aside, I have taken the liberty of enclosing some of my sketches, and would very much appreciate your thoughts. You will note that I have worked hard to maintain some of the more traditional elements of the mace, whilst infusing it (the mace) with a more modern 'feel'.

I look forward to hearing from you,

Best wishes,

Robin Cooper

Robin Cooper

MACES, BY ROBIN COOPER, 2004

KEY (TO MACES)

1. Dual-pointed peak
2. Clasp of Llewellyn
3. 'Pivot' joint.
4. Cast iron through-box
5. Lembitt
6. Knuckle
7. Rounded secondary grip
8. Girdet
9. Handle
10. Silvered scimitar edge
11. Reinforced teeth'
12. Lembitt
13. Prismic through-box
14. Double Knuckle
15. Platform No.1
16. Platform No.2
17. Platform No.3
18. Handle
19. Inverted Cap
20. St George's Podium
21. Triple columned taper
22. Lembittinas
23. Oral support
24. Profile of Lord Haverby
25. Handle
26. Crown of Tocom
27. Curved Clasp
28. Gap
29. Lembitt
30. Prismic through-box
31. Galvanised Tenvits
32. 'Bootie'
33. Galvanised Tenvits
34. Handle

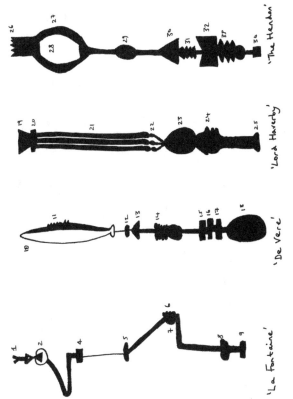

'La Fontaine'   'De Vere'   'Lord Haverby'   'The Henin'

149

THE LONDON MAYORS ASSOCIATION

[Established in 1901]

Chairman: The Lord Mayor of Westminster

President: Hon Alderman Mrs Margaret Calcott-James   Executive Chairman: Councillor Robert Davis

8 Bentinck Street, London W1U 2BJ

Robin Cooper Esq
Brondesbury Villas
London

19th January 2004

Dear Mr Cooper

Thank you for your letter of 15th January 2004 and for enclosing the interesting designs for Mayoral Maces.

Would you give me permission to publish this in our forthcoming Newsletter (if there is room)?

I await to hear from you.

Yours sincerely

COUNCILLOR ROBERT DAVIS
EXECUTIVE CHAIRMAN
THE LONDON MAYORS' ASSOCIATION

RD/SM/LMA4/Jan/59c

**The London Mayors' Association is a Company limited by guarantee
and registered under company number: 3682500**

Robin Cooper
Brondesbury Villas
London

Councillor Robert Davis
Executive Chairman
The London Mayors' Association
c/o Freeman Box & Co
8 Bentinck Street
London W1U 2BJ

4th March 2004

Dear Councillor Robert Davis,

Again I must thank you heartily for your swift reply (19th January) to my letter (15th January), following your reply (14th January) to my letter (7th January). In short – 4 letters in 3 weeks!

You can be sure that I will be spreading the word as to the efficiency of your organisation. Many thanks, once again.

I was delighted that you found my designs 'interesting' and would be only too pleased for you to publish them in your Newsletter.

Would you be so kind as to forward me a copy of your Newsletter. It would make me (and hopefully my wife!) most proud.

I look forward to hearing from you,

Best mace-bearing wishes!

Robin Cooper

DIARY

Tour of Arsenal Football Ground

WEDNESDAY 30TH JUNE 2004
NOON TO 2PM

Tour the world famous Highbury Stadium home of Arsenal Football Club. See behind the scenes, visit the changing rooms, the Marble Hall, the Club Museum and see the Trophy Cabinet. Please complete the application form enclosed and send it to Mrs Helen Watson, 7 Highview Court, 57A Augustus Road, London SW19 6LU.

Meet the Magic Circle

WEDNESDAY 7TH JULY 2004
7.30PM TO 10.30PM

Join the London Mayors' Association for a unique evening of Magic at the world famous Magic Circle. Following a welcome reception, members will enjoy close-up magic followed by a lecture on the history of magic and the Magic Circle. After an interval for sandwiches and coffee the evening will end with a spectacular stage show. The cost will be £30.00 per person. Please complete the application form enclosed and send it to Robert Davis at 8 Bentinck Street London W1U 2BJ.

Visit the Royal Air Force Air Traffic Control Base at West Drayton

MONDAY 12TH JULY 2004
12.30PM TO 5.15PM

Arrangements have been made for a limited number of LMA Members to visit the Royal Air Force Air Traffic Control Base at West Drayton, Middlesex on Monday 12 July 2004. The cost will be £25.00 per head. The visit will start with a buffet lunch served at 12.30pm. After the tour members will make their way to Hillingdon Town Hall for tea to be hosted by the Mayor of Hillingdon. Please complete the application form enclosed and send it to Mrs Helen Watson, 7 Highview Court, 57A Augustus Road, London SW19 6LU.

Annual Civic Service in Westminster Abbey

SUNDAY 24TH OCTOBER 2004 – 3PM

The pomp and ceremony of the Annual Civic Service of the London Mayors' Association will again be held in Westminster Abbey on Sunday 24th October 2004. Further details will be available in the next newsletter but please put the date in your diary.

THE LONDON MAYORS' ASSOCIATION

www.londonmayors.org.uk

8 Bentinck Street London W1U 2BJ

With Compliments

Councillor Robert Davis
Executive Chairman of the London Mayors' Association

The Modern Mace

Robin Cooper has designed a series of modern Maces and with his permission we publish some of them.

'La Fontaine'   'De Vere'   'Lord Haverby'   'The Henken'

Robin Cooper
Brondesbury Villas
London

Roger Millward
Honorary Secretary
The British Button Society
Hawkesworth Drive
Worle
Weston-super-Mare
Somerset

5th January 2004

Dear Mr Millward,

I wonder if you can help. I need some advice from someone who knows all about buttons.

For the past three months, I have been having a recurring dream. I have it at night. In it, a giant turquoise button lands in my back garden. Not only can it walk (it moves about on wheels), it can also talk. In my dream, the button - its name is Hoolarmahan - warns me not to talk to my family again, or I will be taken away to the "Hoolarmahan Zimanoif".

My life at home has become unbearable as I have not uttered a word to my wife or children for six weeks. They think I'm mad. Maybe I am mad. It seems only Hoolarmahan knows the answer.

As a button man yourself, do you feel it is safe for me to ignore Hoolarmahan, and talk to my family again? And what exactly is the "Hoolarmahan Zimanoif"?

Please write back soon.

Many thanks.

Yours sincerely,

R. Li Co

Robin Cooper

NO RESPONSE

Robin Cooper
Brondesbury Villas
London

Mr Tim Cotress
Honorable Secretary
The British Confectioners' Association
Home Farm Business Centre
Brighton
E Sussex

7th January 2004

Dear Mr Cotress,

A friend (who shall remain nameless) of mine told me about your organisation, The British Confectioners' Association. I don't need to tell you that though (i.e spell out the name of your organisation) as you already know it (if you didn't you'd be out of a job) (or demoted!).

Anyway, I think it's fantastic that there is a group DEDICATED to keeping the whole range of confectionery (biscuits, cakes, chocolates etc.) under one metaphorical umbrella. In other words what I'm trying to tell you (in no uncertain words) is that what you are doing is to be PRAISED. Award yourself a gold star Mr Cotress!

I was so impressed by what your organisation, The British Confectioners…(we won't go into that again eh!) is doing (i.e allying biscuits, cakes, chocolates…here we go again – again!) that I want to tell you what I did (because of your inspiration).

Yesterday I went out and bought £450 worth of biscuit, £290 worth of cake, £320 worth of chocolate and £260 worth of confect. I then arranged all the bits in the shape of a giant lizard to signify the severity of reptilian justice metered out by the lizard corporals of the law, who ravage this land with their lengthy tongues of wrath.

In three weeks' time (Friday January 30th), I plan to relocate my giant £1320 lizard model to outside your premises. I will then stamp all over it whilst dressed as a Mini Roll.

I really think that this would be an ideal way to promote your organisation (The British Confectioners Association), and with your permission I would like to invite the world's media along.

If you have any doubts about the idea, please do write back before the three week period is over.

Yours truly,

Robin Cooper

Robin Cooper

154

THE BRITISH CONFECTIONERS' ASSOCIATION

President:
MARTIN WIENHOLT
Chairman:
RICHARD WATERFIELD

Home Farm Road
Home Farm Business Centre,
Brighton

Hon. Treasurer &
Hon. Secretary:
TIM CUTRESS

Robin Cooper
Brondesbury Villas
London

13th January 2004

Dear Mr Cooper

I am in receipt of your letter of 7th January and note your contents.

Obviously your nameless friend knows very little about the BCA, or he would have been able to advise you that the above address is not that of our headquarters, but my own bakery used as the postal address for the association!

Our membership consists of 60 elected members, all of whom run small to medium sized bakery business's throughout the UK. We meet five times a year to exchange ideas and visit members and other retail and production premises.

I suggest that your giant lizard and Mini roll would attract far greater publicity if carried out at a more high profile location!

Yours truly

Tim Cutress
Hon Secretary

END OF CORRESPONDENCE

155

Robin Cooper
Brondesbury Villas
London

Arthur Roberts
Secretary
Friends of Blue
Coscote
Didcot
Oxon

7th January 2004

Dear Mr Roberts,

I wonder if you can help.

My daughter, Lisa, is Blue mad. She has all their records (including 'pirate' discs – please don't tell the police!), and their posters cover all 4 walls of her bedroom – including half the ceiling!

The reason I am writing is that I would be very grateful if you could send me a signed photo of the band. It would mean so much to my daughter.

As it is the 5th anniversary of her temporal verification graduation, I wonder if the lads could write the following short message to her:

Dear Lisa,

Congratulations on the 5th anniversary of your temporal verification graduation. We trust that you will continue to verify all matters concerning the passing of time, according to the laws governing Greenwich and all her affiliates.

Yours,

(Insert band member's names here)

Thank you so much in advance. I enclose a S.A.E.

Best wishes,

Robin Cooper

Robin Cooper

Sorry unable to help.
Friends of Blue members are
interested in antique blue and
white transfer printed pottery.
Not quite Lisa's scene!

Arthur Roberts

END OF CORRESPONDENCE

156

Robin Cooper
Brondesbury Villas
London

Lynn B Snead
The British Luggage and Leather Goods Association
Vyse Street
Birmingham

16th February 2004

Dear Lynn B Snead,

I wonder if you can help.

My wife recently purchased a leather bag about a year ago from a store in London.

At the time of purchase, there was nothing that indicated that the bag would bring us so much misfortune in so little time….

Here is the catalogue of events that have occurred since purchase:

1) Wife's bad ankle weakened. New dressing needs to be applied on a regular basis.
2) Ceiling in shed buckled under weight of neighbour's cat 'Tiggles'.
3) Car broke down just two metres from the garage. Two metres!
4) Daughter (Lisa) consistently forgot to clean pans after use.
5) Insurance form returned, as I had failed to complete it correctly (left off date of birth).

As a leading light in the luggage world, do you think there is something about the bag that could have caused all of this?

The bag is 20 cm in length, 10 cm high, and 8 cm deep. It is hewn in dark brown leather, with the brand 'Kempof 19/C' stitched prominently all over it.

Can you help?

I look forward to hearing from you,

With very best wishes,

R. Li Cor

Robin Cooper

The
**British Luggage
and Leathergoods**
Association

Mr. R. Cooper
Bronsbury Villas
London

24th February, 2004

Dear Mr Cooper

Thank you for your letter of 16 February. I see that you feel that your family has experienced a lot of bad luck since purchasing a leather bag about a year ago, but I think that you may have experienced a lot of good luck instead.

I have no explanations as to why you should have received so much bad luck with the bag, let's just hope the next year will be 'all good luck'

Many thanks for your enquiry to the BLLA.

Yours sincerely

Diana Fiveash
BLLA

Robin Cooper
Brondesbury Villas
London

Diana Fiveash
The British Luggage and Leather Goods Association
Vyse Street
Birmingham

2nd March 2004

Dear Diana,

Many thanks for your letter of 24th February. Whatever happened to Lynn B Snead by the way?

Your letter certainly went some way in cheering me (and my wife) up, so it is with hearty gratitude that I am writing/typing this letter. I thank you once again.

In fact, since receiving your letter, things have started to get better...

At the weekend I was sent a free ream of A4 paper from an anonymous benefactor, and yesterday, Tiggles, the neighbour's cat who damaged my shed, was sent to a cattery – for life.

Thus, you may be right – the good times may be about to roll!

I thank you once again, for taking the time to write.

May I ask, is there any gift you may fancy in recompense?

I look forward to hearing from you.

With best wishes,

Robin Cooper

The
**British Luggage
and Leathergoods**
Association

Mr. R. Cooper,
Brondesbury Villas,
London

9th March, 2004

Dear Robin,

Thank you for your letter of 2nd March, 2004. I am pleased that things have started to get better for you both. Amazing what a new month brings.

It's a mystery for you to receive a ream of A4 paper, very nice too. Tiggles, the cat, will have been put out of his misery – especially if he was damaging your shed regularly.

Regarding a gift, well how about a little more 'sunshine', that would be nice.

Lynn Snead still works for the British Jewellery and Giftware Federation, but not for the BLLA, she works for the Benevolent Society on a part-time basis and works from home.

I did pass your letter on to her for her personal viewing. Were you in the luggage or leathergoods industry previously, how did you know Lynn?

Many thanks for your letter and hope the year improves for you both.

With best wishes.

Kind regards

Diana Fiveash
Chief Executive
BLLA

Robin Cooper
Brondesbury Villas
London

Diana Fiveash
The British Luggage and Leather Goods Association
Vyse Street
Birmingham

15th March 2004

Dear Diana,

Thank you for your lovely letter of 9th March in reaction to mine of 2nd March. It was both greatly and heartily accepted – with gratitude!!!

Yes, I am pleased to be rid, at last, of Tiggles. He was a cat of ill deed and wickedness, although in his defence, I did once spy him comforting his master and mistress after they had discovered a wasp's nest in their attic, so there's hope for us all!

You asked about how I knew Lynn Snead. In actual fact, I don't, merely her name was the one that was passed on to me (by Lord Poynton) as the best contact for your organisation. I apologise for any confusion caused thereof.

You also asked whether I was in the luggage or leathergoods industry. Sadly, I regret to say that I have never been in the luggage or leathergoods business.

In the meantime, I am sending you a spot of sunshine within this letter. Did you like it?

I look forward to hearing from you, and enclose a SAE.

With best wishes,

Robin Cooper

Robin Cooper

END OF CORRESPONDENCE

Robin Cooper
Brondesbury Villas
London

Derek A Edwards
Chairman
The National Association of Aerial Photographic Libraries
Lansdown House
Breton Close
Toftwood
East Dereham
Norfolk
NR19 1JH

26th February 2004

Dear Mr Edwards,

Phew – not quite a record but pretty close! I am of course referring to the fact that you have 9 lines in your address!

Please excuse my little joke, and I trust you are well, though we have never met. However I wonder if you can help.

I am a keen aerial photographer and have been taking photos (on a semi-professional basis) for about 7 years. Whilst I have only sold a handful of my prints (several to Lord Foulton, plus a couple to Sally de Mimes), I now own one of the largest collection of photographs of aerials in Britain.

At the latest count I have over 4,500 photos, ranging from standard television aerials to the celebrated Montefiore transmitter aerial in Somerset.

Would your organisation be interested in holding copies of my photographs, for posterity as it were?

Many thanks in advance, and I look forward to hearing from you.

Best wishes,

Robin Cooper

An independent organisation
promoting the use and
preservation of aerial photographs

Mr R Cooper
Brondesbury Villas
London

2 March 2004

Dear Mr Cooper,

Thank you for your letter of 26 February, which has been forwarded to me by Derek Edwards, our former chairman.

I am sorry to say that we are unable to help you. While the names of our respective interests are similar, the subject matter is entirely different. While you are involved in the photography of aerials, NAPLIB is devoted to aerial photographs, that is, photographs of the ground taken from the air.

Yours sincerely,

Kevin McLaren
Honorary Secretary

Robin Cooper
Brondesbury Villas
London

Kevin McLaren
Honorary Secretary
The National Association of Aerial Photographic Libraries
Lansdown House
Breton Close
Toftwood
East Dereham
Norfolk
NR19 1JH

4th March 2004

Dear Mr McLaren,

Many thanks for your letter of 2nd March.

I would like to apologise deeply for the confusion caused over my lack of understanding as to how the term 'aerial' is applied to your organisation.

I now realise that aerial photographs (i.e. photographs of aerials) do not fall within your remit, whereas aerial photographs (i.e. photographs taken from the air) do. Thus, would you perhaps be interested in my collection of aerial photographs of aerials? That is, aerial photographs (photographs taken from the air), of aerials?

I look forward to hearing from you

Many thanks again, and once more, apologies.

Best wishes,

Robin Cooper

Mr R Cooper
Brondesbury Villas
London

10 March 2004

Dear Mr Cooper,

Thank you for your letter of 4 March, which has been forwarded to me by Derek Edwards, our former chairman. Please note the new contact address for NAPLIB, which appears at the foot of this page.

Confusion over the use of the word aerial is entirely understandable, given our respective specialisms. NAPLIB does not itself hold collections of aerial photographs, being simply an association of organisations which do hold such material. However, it does produce a members newsletter, where it might be possible to place a small article on your collection in the next issue. In this way, any member libraries or individuals interested in your subject matter could be made aware of your collection. I would be happy to forward any such article you may wish to write to our editor for consideration.

Yours sincerely,

Kevin McLaren
Honorary Secretary

Robin Cooper
Brondesbury Villas
London

Kevin McLaren
Honorary Secretary
The National Association of Aerial Photographic Libraries
Lansdown House
Breton Close
Toftwood
East Dereham
Norfolk
NR19 1JH

16th March 2004

Dear Mr McLaren,

I am in receipt of your letter of 10th March, and thank you heartily for it.

I would indeed be interested in penning a small article for inclusion in your newsletter, and I hereby enclose it herewin.

Aerial Aerials by Robin Cooper

There can be some confusion regarding the term 'aerial'. I, myself, am an aerial photographer, however, not one who specialises in taking pictures from the air, no, rather one who takes pictures of aerials (TV, radio etc.). I now have one of the largest collections in the UK, (over 4,500 at the last count), second only to Sir Michael Hembrose (6,250).

A few years back, however, I became interested in the notion of taking aerial photographs of aerials. That is aerial photographs (photographs from the air) of aerials (on the ground, roof tops, building tops etc.).

I am lucky enough to have use of a helicopter at the weekends, and every now and then I fly out to Somerset, home of the famous Montefiore transmitter, or to Hull, to aerially photograph the celebrated Hinberry-Stross aerial, atop the town's swimming baths.

The pictures are fascinating to develop. The aerials appear flat, jagged, mysterious, somewhat resembling deep fissures, like those seen through a microscope, whence pondering a piece of quartz or material torn from an umbrella.

So the next time you meet an aerial photographer. Think twice. It may be me!

I wonder if you would be so kind as to publish this. I look forward to hearing from you.

Best wishes,

Robin Cooper

Robin Cooper

END OF CORRESPONDENCE

Robin Cooper
Brondesbury Villas
London

Peter Bryant
Honorary Secretary
The Confederation of Long Distance Racing Pigeons Union of Great Britain and
Ireland
The Reddings
Cheltenham
Glos. GL51 6RN

27th February 2004

Dear Mr Bryant,

Phew! What a wide address! It occupies the whole width of the page!

But that is beside the point and of scant interest to you, I am sure.

I have been breeding racing pigeons for approx. a decade. I say 'approx.' as I mean
'approximately' but I think you can see what I mean!

Anyway, during these 9 years of breeding (pigeons) I have bred a wonderful line of
birds that are able to fly great distances and at great speed.

Here are the latest results:

Name of Pigeon	Distance	Time
'Paleface'	710 miles	3 days
'Billy Boy'	660 miles	3 days
'Taul-Polip'	500 miles	4 days
'Mr King'	490 miles	15 days
'Frinley'	305 miles	20 days

In your experience, would I (or rather THEY – the PIGEONS) qualify for any
medals/prizes/records?

I look forward to hearing from you.

Happy flapping!

Robin Coop

Robin Cooper

THE ROYAL PIGEON RACING ASSOCIATION
Patron : Her Majesty the Queen
Affiliated to the Federation Colombophile Internationale

Reddings House
The Reddings
Near Cheltenham
Gloucestershire
GL51 6RN

PNRB/MAC/LONDON
Our Reference

2ND March, 2004

Mr. R. Cooper
Brondesbury Villas
London

Dear Mr Cooper

Thank you for your letter regarding prizes for your pigeons.

Sadly, I think your pigeons have a way to go before they are able to compete against prize winners of the Royal Pigeon Racing Association.

Our furthest race to the UK is from Barcelona, some 700 miles for most fanciers and the winning bird is likely to take about 20 hours maximum.

Happy flapping indeed!

Yours sincerely,

Peter Bryant
General Manager.

END OF CORRESPONDENCE

Robin Cooper
Brondesbury Villas
London

The Campaign for Courtesy
The Avenue
Basford
Newcastle-Upon-Lyme
Staffs.

16th February 2004

Dear Sir/Madam,

I trust that this letter finds you in good spirits.

I have heard many good things about your wonderful organisation, and would be
honoured if you would be so kind as to let me tell you of my own, personal ideas as to
how to make Britain more courteous.

Would you (care to hear of the above)?

I look forward to hearing from you.

With very best wishes,

In yours, I remain,

R. Li Coop

Robin Cooper

Campaign for Courtesy

The Reverend Ian Gregory
Grice Road
Hartshill
Stoke-on-Trent

Feb 23 '04

Dear Mr Cooper

Thanks for your vote We are always interested in ideas, whoever they come from, to create a more Courteous UK. Please let me know what you think

Yours sincerely

Ian Gregory

170

Robin Cooper
Brondesbury Villas
London

The Reverend Ian Gregory
The Campaign for Courtesy
Grice Road
Hartshill
Stoke-on-Trent

26th February 2004

Dear Reverend Gregory,

Hearty thanks for your charming letter of three days yonder.

I was delighted that you were interested in some of my ideas as to how to make Britain more courteous. They are as follows:

<u>Robin Cooper 10 Point Plan for a Courteous Britain:</u>

1) Always address your elders as 'Sir' or 'Madam'
2) Never talk with your mouth open
3) Do not lean across people at mealtimes
4) All citizens must wear a badge bearing their family crest on formal occasions (such as All Saint's Day, Queen's Birthday etc)
5) Swearing, or uncouth behaviour, to be punished by reduction of state pension (on a sliding scale according to severity of offence)
6) All men over the age of 18 to wear brimmed hats on Sundays
7) Children under 18 to be kept indoors after 7pm at weekends
8) Voting age to be raised to 21
9) Pointing at people to be punishable by on the spot fines
10) The National Anthem to be played at all workplaces at beginning and end of working day.

That, in a nutshell, is my plan. Are you interested in championing it? I was thinking of getting some leaflets printed bearing your name and likeness if possible.

I look forward to hearing from you.

In yours, I remain,

Robin Cooper

END OF CORRESPONDENCE

Robin Cooper
Brondesbury Villas
London

John A Stinton
The British Cleaning Council
PO Box 1328
Kidderminster
Worcs DY11 5ZJ

27th February 2004

Dear Mr Stinton,

I wonder if you would be interested in my little venture.

Each year I hold a contest with one of my neighbours to see who can clean their abode the fastest. We call the contest 'Nicolas Alfonso's Super Benefaction'. It's been running for 4 years now (5 once we've done this year's one).

How it works is this: my neighbour (Peter La Rosse) and I first spend 30 minutes 'dirtying' each other's homes using agreed materials – usually soil, animal fat, congealed milk and sawdust. However, nothing in either house must be damaged or broken.

Once this has been done, the contest begins. The winner is the person who has the cleanest house in the fastest time.

We have had extensive coverage in the local paper, and wonder if your organisation would care to sponsor us? We would be looking to raise somewhere in the region of £2,000 (mainly to cover repairs etc.). In return we would don British Cleaning Council t-shirts, or use rags emblazoned with your logo for example.

Would this be something you would be interested in?

I look forward to hearing from you.

Best wishes,

Robin Cooper

Robin Cooper

PS - The next Nicolas Alfonso's Super Benefaction takes place on Saturday March 27th. Mr La Rosse and I have both won twice, so this year promises to be very exciting.

British Cleaning Council

BCC Limited Reg. Nº 2128175
P.O. Box 1328, Kidderminster, Worcestershire. DY11 5ZJ

01 March 2004

Robin Cooper
Brondesbury Villa
LONDON

Dear Mr Cooper

Thank you for your letter of the 27th February.

The British Cleaning Council awards funding to and through member Associations. Each application is presented to Council by the Association making the request. Your venture is outside of the aims and objectives of the British Cleaning Council and therefore I am sorry that we cannot support your request.

I hope your little venture is a success.

I have enclosed details of the BCC Ltd and the member Associations for your information.

Kind regards.

Yours sincerely,

John A Stinton
Company Secretary and Treasurer.

END OF CORRESPONDENCE

Robin Cooper
Brondesbury Villas
London

Mr M J Dellar
Secretary
The Envelope Makers' & Manufacturing Stationers' Association
Church View
Church Lane
Arrington
Royston
Herts

3rd March 2004

Dear Mr Dellar,

I am planning a surprise slide show for a neighbour, Tony Sutton, who has just recovered from a broken shin after he slipped on some rotten meat.

My presentation will be all about envelopes. I have found it quite tricky to get good research on this subject, and unfortunately I am not hooked up to the intanet. I would therefore be most grateful if you could spare a couple of minutes of your time to answer a few of my questions. I shall of course be enclosing a SAE.

QUESTIONS:

1) Who invented the envelope?
2) Was it, like penicillin, (the discovery of) an accident?
3) How many envelopes are there in circulation?
4) What is the largest envelope ever made?
5) What is the most expensive envelope in the world?
6) How much does it cost?
7) Where does one safely dispose of envelopes?
8) Has there ever been any poetry written about envelopes?

I would like to thank you in advance for all your help. I am holding the surprise slide show in April. If you are interested in attending, I would be more than happy to send you tickets.

Best wishes,

Robin Cooper

The Envelope Makers' & Manufacturing Stationers' Association.

Director : Michael J. Dellar.
Church View, Church Lane, Arrington, Royston, Herts

17th March 2004

Mr. R. Cooper,
Brondesbury Villas,
London

Dear Mr Cooper,

Thank you for your letter concerning the slide show that you are developing for your neighbour. I can only agree that envelopes are not a particularly well documented subject.

I regret that I am unable to provide answers to a number of questions as I have never seen any details of the most expensive envelope or if any poetry has been written about envelopes. However I enclose an article that I have located which I think will be of interest and gives details of the origin of envelopes. On the subject of the largest envelope I enclose an item that I have obtained from a colleague that we believe may answer this for you.

I do not know how many envelopes there are in circulation but as a start point Royal Mail handle approximately 84 million letters each working day.

Envelopes can easily be re-cycled if they are made of paper and increasingly Councils are collecting them.

I hope that this is of assistance and I wish you every success with your venture.

Yours sincerely,

M.J.Dellar

END OF CORRESPONDENCE

175

Robin Cooper
Brondesbury Villas
London

Lost Property Office
Debenhams Superstore
334-348 Oxford Street
London
W1C 1JG

3rd March 2004

Dear Sir/Madam,

I am writing to you for help.

I visited your store last Saturday 28th February. Whilst in the linen department, browsing at duvet covers, I appear to have lost the lace from my right shoe (brogue).

I wonder if anyone has handed it in? It's black, about two years old and roughly 25 centimetres long.

Perhaps you have it on close circuit camera? My wife has told me not to hold out too much hope for my missing lace and even suggested buying another one, but it's just not the same is it?

I would be most grateful if you could write back to me ASAP and tell me one way or the other if you have it or not. That way you can put me out of my misery and I can begin to carry on with my life.

I look forward to your reply.

Yours faithfully,

Robin Cooper

DEBENHAMS

PO BOX 16
334-348 OXFORD STREET
LONDON W1C 1JG
TELEPHONE 020 7580 3000
FACSIMILE 020 7518 7408
www.debenhams.com

Mr Robin Cooper
Brondesbury Villas
London

6th. March 2004

Dear Mr Cooper

Thank you, for your letter regarding your lost shoelace.

I have checked our lost property log and unfortunately nothing has been handed in to us.

If I can be of any further assistance in this or any other matter please do not hesitate to contact me as detailed.

Yours sincerely

Ian Staines
Sales Manager Customer service

Debenhams Retail plc, a member of the Debenhams plc Group of Companies. Registered in England. Company no. 83395. Registered office 1 Welbeck Street, London W1G 0AA.

Ian Staines
Sales Manager Customer Service
Debenhams Superstore
334-348 Oxford Street
London
W1C 1JG

10th March 2004

Dear Mr Staines,

Many thanks for your letter of 6th March 2004 regarding the loss of my shoelace during my visit to Debenhams Superstore on Saturday 28th February 2004.

Whilst I appreciate your efforts, I was absolutely distraught when I read that you were unable to find it anywhere in the store. I do hope you appreciate that this is much more than just a shoelace to me - it's an air loom.

The best solution is for me and you to have a good look for it together, so I will meet you in the linen department on Friday 26th March at 1:00pm. Please make sure the department is closed for at least half an hour while we look for my missing property.

If there are any problems please get in touch, otherwise I'll see you on the 26th (you'll recognise me, as I will be bringing my dogs along to help in the search).

Until then,

Robin Cooper

DEBENHAMS

PO BOX 16
334-348 OXFORD STREET
LONDON W1C 1JG
TELEPHONE 020 7580 3000
FACSIMILE 020 7518 7408
www.debenhams.com

Mr R. Cooper
Brondesbury Villas
London

11th. March 2004

Dear Mr Cooper

Thank you once again for your correspondence regarding your lost shoe lace.

I understand that the loss is causing you great concern and therefore of course I would like to do all that is possible to assist you in bringing this matter to a close.

I have re checked the linen department this morning unfortunately without success. Due to our high cleaning standards I am very confident that your shoe lace is not any where in our store.

However if you would like to come in and look of course you are welcome to do so. Regrettably I cannot close a department for half an hour while the store is open however if you would like to search without interruption I would be happy to assist you when the store is closed. If you would like to let me know a date we can meet at the information desk on the ground floor shortly before we close at 8.00pm. When we have cleared the store myself or a member of the team will be happy to escort you around. Unfortunately we will not be able to let any dogs except registered guide dogs into the store. May I suggest that the sooner you are able to come in the higher the chance of success.

I look forward to hearing from you if this offer is acceptable.

Yours sincerely

Ian Staines

Sales Manager Customer service

Debenhams Retail plc, a member of the Debenhams plc Group of Companies. Registered in England. Company no. 83395. Registered office 1 Welbeck Street, London W1G 0AA.

Robin Cooper
Brondesbury Villas
London

Ian Staines
Sales Manager Customer Service
Debenhams Superstore
334-348 Oxford Street
London
W1C 1JG

15th March 2004

Dear Mr Staines,

RE: LOST SHOELACE.

Wow! What service! I am of course referring to your letter of 11th March regarding the above two words following the abbreviation 'Re'.

I thank you. It is nothing short of what I would have expected from such a wonderful organisation/retail outlet as Debenhams. Now I know why everyone calls you(r) (place of work) a 'superstore'. It really is a SUPER store!

I read your letter with interest and I would be pleased to take you up on your kind offer. Would it be possible for me to attend your store on Monday April 12th at 7:55 pm, with the aim of locating my shoelace?

I look forward to hearing from you.

Best wishes,

Robin Cooper

Robin Cooper

PS – I do understand your 'no dogs' policy, however, will I be allowed to bring along my hamster 'Hambles' (whom I will keep in his portable hutch at all times, this I swear) to assist in the search? Hambles has an incredible sense of smell, which is 5 times more powerful than that of a human – and 5 noses have got to be better than one!

END OF CORRESPONDENCE

Robin Cooper
Brondesbury Villas
London

Vivian Thornton Linacre
Director
The British Weights & Measures Association
Montgomery Street
Edinburgh

3rd March 2004

Dear Vivian,

Away with this ridiculum! Be off with you! Good day!

Just some of the things I not only dreamt about last night but repeated mantra-form, as soon as I awoke.

I'm talking of course about weights and measures and the whole 'metric nonsense'. Why must we be SLAVES to those that would ENSLAVEN us (in relation to weights and measures – i.e. centimetres v kilogrammes etc. etc. ad infinititum).

Thus I present myself, Robin Cooper, ready to aid thee in thy quest for a return to civility and non-metric weights and measures.

In other words, I am at your service, my Liege.

I have several new ways of helping you in your conquest.

Care to be enlightened?

I look forward to hearing from you.

Privy thee,

[signature]

Robin Cooper

Marshall Place, Perth   **VIVIAN LINACRE**
Fellow: Royal Society for the Arts   Fellow: Institute of Contemporary Scotland
President: British Weights and Measures Association

18 · iii · 04

Dear Robin Cooper

MANY THANKS FOR YOUR LETTER OF 3RD MARCH — REDIRECTED FROM MY OLD ADDRESS.

HEREWITH A (FREE!) COPY OF THE NEW ISSUE OF 'THE YARDSTICK'.

DO PLEASE ATTEND OUR AGM & CONFERENCE ON 22ND MAY.

MEANWHILE, OF COURSE, BECOME A MEMBER BY SENDING YOUR DETAILS WITH A £10.00 CHEQUE TO OUR HON. TREASURER.

BY ALL MEANS TELEPHONE ME IF YOU WISH TO DISCUSS FURTHER. [YOU DID NOT GIVE A TEL. No.!]

Sincerely

Vivian Linacre

END OF CORRESPONDENCE

182

Robin Cooper
Brondesbury Villas
London

Keith M Taylor
Director
The British Wild Boar Association
PO Box 100
London W6 0ZJ

3rd March 2004

Dear Mr Taylor,

Greetings from one wild boar lover to another!

I have been studying boars and their behaviour for a very long time now, although too long for me to actually remember the precise start date of my studies, which was August 9th 1990.

Along the way I have devoted much of my time to designing the optimum living space for a boar. And now I think I have it.

I have created the 'Boar'ngalow' – a single floored dwelling, constructed from wood, with enough room for boar maneouvre and general boar-related recreational activities (sleeping, mating, gnawing etc).

Would you care to see a 'sneak preview' of the Boar'ngalow, before it appears in a very high-profile scientific magazine?

I look forward to hearing from you.

With very best wishes,

Robin Cooper

The British Wild Boar Association

To promote the commercial development, welfare and understanding of husbanded wild boar in Britain

P.O. Box 100
London W6 0ZJ

9 March, 2004

Mr. Robin Cooper
Brondesbury Villas
London

Dear Mr. Cooper,

'BOAR'NGALOW'

Thank you for your most interesting letter of 3 March. What prompted you to create such a product and do you intend to exploit it commercially? Have you built a prototype and put a boar(s) into it in 'field' conditions? They are very 'hard' on equipment and also destructive – have you given it any life cycle testing? What would it cost to buy one?

Yes, I would like a 'sneak preview' – the article might have increased credibility if it has been examined/tested by a wild boar farmer. Has it and if not perhaps we could arrange something.

Please call me.

Yours sincerely,

Keith M. Taylor
<u>Director</u>

Robin Cooper
Brondesbury Villas
London

Keith M Taylor
Director
The British Wild Boar Association
PO Box 100
London W6 0ZJ

15th March 2004

Dear Mr Taylor,

RE: BOAR'NGALOW

Hearty thanks for your letter of 9th March, in response to mine of 6 days previous. I am very sorry that I have not been able to call you, as I am currently unable to use the telephone.

You asked me a number of questions regarding the Boar'ngalow, and I herewin take great pleasure in attempting to answer them.

1) "What prompted you (me) to create such a product?".
I once owned a wild boar called 'Wilson' who lived in my garden shed. Unfortunately, within a week, Wilson destroyed the entire shed (although this was not helped by my neighbour's cat, Tiggles, who, attracted to Wilson's scent, kept jumping on the roof, which slowly began to buckle in). I set upon designing a new dwelling for Wilson. This became the Boar'ngalow.
2) "Do you (me) intend to exploit it commercially?".
Anything that is good for boars is good for me, however if it makes me a millionaire, then so be it.
3) "Have you (me) built a prototype and put a boar(s) into it in 'field' conditions?".
Yes, I have built a prototype. At present a wild boar named 'Camfy' lives inside. Camfy is a very happy boar in there.
4) "Have you (me) given it any life cycle testing?".
Please elaborate. Sadly, I do not understand the question.
5) "What would it cost to buy one?".
Not sure yet. As a wild boar man yourself, what would you pay for one?
6) "Has [it] been examined/tested by a wild boar farmer?".
Yes, by a gentleman named Charlie Heppington. It passed with flying colours!

I do trust my answers help clarify things. Would you care to see a sketch of the Boar'ngalow?

I look forward to hearing from you.

Best wishes,

Robin Cooper

END OF CORRESPONDENCE

The Director
The Ashphalt Industry Alliance
Eccleston Street
London

6th March 2004

Dear Sir/Madam,

Allow me to introduce myself...

I have been working within the asphalt industry for over a dozen years, and have decided to give something back to the asphalt world, a world which, I must admit, has been a kind mistress (to me).

With that in mind, I have set upon developing a Light and Sound show that both entertains and educates the public about the benefits of working within the asphalt industry.

Would you care to hear more of this?

I thank you for your time, and look forward to hearing from you.

Kindest of regards,

Robin Cooper

**ASPHALT
INDUSTRY
ALLIANCE**

Robin Cooper
Brondesbury Villas
London

AIA Press Office
Eccleston Street
London

12 March 2004

Dear Mr Cooper,

Thank you for your letter dated 6 March 2004. Your Light and Sound show sounds
very interesting, and we would like to hear more about this project.

Please could you telephone me on the above number to give me some more
details? I am interested to hear the purpose of and reason behind your undertaking.

I look forward to hearing from you.

Yours sincerely,

Jen Stebbing
Asphalt Press Office

Robin Cooper
Brondesbury Villas
London

Jen Stebbing
Asphalt Press Office
The Ashphalt Industry Alliance
Eccleston Street
London

16th March 2004

Dear Jen,

Thank you ever so much for your charming letter of 12th March (the date, incidentally, of my mother's birthday!).

But that is, sadly, irrelevant.

I would very much like to telephone you, but unfortunately I am unable to use the telephone at the moment, due to reasons *non dimentares ultraltimus*. I trust you understand.

However, I should be able to enlighten you a little regarding my proposed Light and Sound Show.

I have worked with both asphalt and lasers for many years, and so have good contacts in both fields. Hence, I am able to get hold of a giant, industrial laser, which, when installed outside or atop your premises, could fire huge letters into the sky. For example, a simple slogan such as: 'A-S-P-H-A-L-T-A-N-I-N-D-U-S-T-R-Y-O-F-A-L-I-F-E-T-I-M-E-A-N-D-A-N-I-N-D-U-S-T-R-Y-F-O-R-L-I-F-E-!', or, 'A-S-P-H-A-L-T-I-S-(-E-V-E-N-T-U-A-L-L-Y-)-C-O-O-L-!'

In the meantime, a crowd would gather and be treated to a demonstration of various asphalting methods and techniques by your staff. They could take part in activities, ranging from measuring the elasticity of pavement layers, to gauging 'buckling' in paving stones.

There will of course be music (provided by 'The Cavershams'), and lots of dancing. Hopefully you'll join in too!

Can you help get this all in motion?

I look forward to hearing from you.

Best wishes,

Robin Cooper

Robin Cooper
Brondesbury Villas
London

18 March 2004

Dear Mr Cooper,

Thank you for your letter of 16 March and the explanation of your proposed Light
and Sound Show.

Unfortunately, it would not be appropriate for the Alliance and so I am afraid we
will not be taking it any further.

Thank you for your interest.

Yours sincerely,

Jen Stebbing

END OF CORRESPONDENCE

Robin Cooper
Brondesbury Villas
London

C Sloan
Director General
The British Refrigeration Association
Henley Road
Medmenham
Marlow
Bucks
SL7 2ER

6th March 2004

Dear Mr Sloan,

I am writing to you for some advice.

My fridge broke down the other day, after my daughter chewed through the mains lead. It was terrible because I was keeping a lovely bit of turkey nice and cool inside.

I have had to take the turkey out of the fridge and it is now sitting on the sideboard in the kitchen.

Can you give me any advice as to how to keep my turkey chilled?

I thank you in advance for your reply.

Keep cool!

Yours sincerely,

Robin Cooper

Mr Cooper,

I regret we are not involved in domestic refrigeration and can not offer the advice you seek.

END OF CORRESPONDENCE

Robin Cooper
Brondesbury Villas
London

The Director
The Royal Festival Hall
Belvedere Road
London SE1 8XX

6th March 2004

Dear Sir/Madam,

We all love music (particularly my wife and I – even with her bad ankle!), indeed I believe it is a pleasure that can and SHOULD be enjoyed by one and all, for that is the LEAST one can do, isn't it?

I am writing to ask you whether it would be possible for my wife and I to perform an 'Evening of Light Music' at your premises in Spring? Although we are both amateur Light Musicians, we always maintain the highest professionalism when dealing with an audience of (mixed) adults.

Here is our proposed programme:

7:00 pm Registration: Guests arrive at the Royal Festival Hall, and are ticked off a list by my wife
7:30 Guests are seated.
7:45 Lights dim and the show begins!
7:46 My wife and I introduce the show (audience must stand throughout)
8:00 Show begins (audience are seated again):
      Song One – Aria from 'La Timerera' by Anthony de Juste
      Song Two – 'Petticoats' by Robin Cooper and The VSX-200
      Performance Three – Lecture by my wife about Light Music
10:00 Interval
10:10 Show continues
      Song Three – 'Petticoats' (reprise) by Robin Cooper and The VSX-200
      Song Four – 'Thou Hast Been Away For Far Too Longe My Love' by Robin Cooper
      Performance Four – Lecture by my wife about Light Music
12:00 am Show ends
12:10 Audience disperse/hall cleared/chairs stacked neatly away

I trust you will agree that this is both a fascinating and varied evening, and that it celebrates Light Music with the RESPECT it should be accorded. Can we arrange?

I look forward to hearing from you – with best wishes naturally!

R. Li Cor

Robin Cooper

Royal Festival Hall
Hayward Gallery
South Bank Centre

Administered on behalf of the Arts Council of England:
Arts Council Collection
National Touring Exhibitions
Saison Poetry Library:
housing The Arts Council Poetry Collection

South Bank Centre
Royal Festival Hall
London SE1 8XX
T +44 (0) 20 7921 0600
F +44 (0) 20 7928 0063
www.southbankcentre.org.uk

Book Online
www.rfh.org.uk
www.hayward.org.uk

Robin Cooper
Brondesbury Villas
London

16th March 04

Dear Mr Cooper

Many thanks for your application to present 'An Evening of Light Music'.

Unfortunately the Purcell Room is fully booked until 2005, and I'm afraid that your event is not the type of show that we programme at the South Bank Centre. We don't ask our audience to stand for a presentation, and usually they have had enough by 10pm, so a midnight finish might be pushing it.

I do hope you find a venue that is suited to you and your wife's show. Please send our best wishes for a speedy recovery for her bad ankle.

Your sincerely

Elspeth McBain
Head of Hall Programme Planning
Royal Festival Hall

END OF CORRESPONDENCE

Music   Dance   Literature   Visual Arts   Education